He made the stars also

What the Bible says about the stars

Stuart Burgess

D1396330

"Both our world and the heavens seem to sparkle with a new identity as a consequence of this book"
— REV GEOFF THOMAS

Day One

© Day One Publications 2001
First printed 2001

All Scripture quotations are taken from The New King James Version.
© International Bible Society. Published by Hodder and Stoughton.

British Library Cataloguing in Publication Data available
ISBN 1 903087 26-0

Published by Day One Publications
3 Epsom Business Park, Kiln Lane, Epsom, Surrey KT17 1JF.
01372 728 300 **FAX** 01372 722 400
email—sales@dayone.co.uk
www.dayone.co.uk

Designed by Steve Devane and printed by Creative Print and Design

For my brother Steve

"By the Word of the Lord the heavens were made, and all
the host of them by the breath of His mouth...For He
spoke, and it was done; He commanded, and it stood fast".

Psalm 33:6–9

Contents

Acknowledgements

I have had help from many colleagues and friends in the course of writing this book. I am particularly grateful for helpful comments on the text from Mr Mike Adams, Professor Don DeYoung, Mr Paul Garner, Dr Russell Healey, Professor Andy McIntosh, Dr Oliver Rice, Mr Nick Shires, Dr Bill Worraker and the editors at DayOne. Any errors or omissions are my responsibility and I would welcome comments from readers.

Dr Stuart Burgess
Department of Mechanical Engineering, Bristol University
Queen's Building, University Walk, Bristol, BS8 1TR

The first words of the Bible are, "In the beginning God created the heaven and the Earth. And the Earth ..." (Genesis 1:1&2). How striking that the Earth is mentioned at the end of verse one *and* the beginning of verse two. My teacher, Professor Edward J Young of Westminster Theological Seminary, Philadelphia, believed that the original has an even stronger emphasis on the Earth. He thought that to better capture the original, the translation of verse two should begin something like this, "Now the Earth..." or "The Earth moreover...".[1]

The initial purpose of the author is to inform us that everything in the universe was created by God. The one living and true God alone made everything that exists. But then the author takes his readers a step further, that henceforth his intention is to focus upon our planet Earth. "No longer is our thought to rest upon the heaven and the Earth, the entirety of created phenomena, but merely upon the Earth".[2] The word 'Earth' is the subject to which attention must be directed, and it is the grand theme, not merely of the remainder of the chapter, but of the remainder of the Bible itself. It is this Earth on which we live with which the Scripture has to do and to which it will direct its thought".[2]

As Professor Aalders has also written, "That the 'Earth' is given a place of emphasis here need not surprise us. This is where we human beings dwell, where we live, suffer and die. Genesis 1:1 informs us that there is more in God's creation than only this Earth. But the Earth is more particularly our domain".[3] So from a contemplation of all created bodies beside our own, the Bible takes a geocentric emphasis, and it maintains that perspective throughout, to its last page. It centres our attention upon this world in which we live, on which we have sinned and to which the Son of God came by incarnation, living long years, dying as the Lamb of God, rising from the dead for our salvation and also for the redemption of a new heaven and Earth.

The Bible could not think of this world in any other way, but the theological centre of the entire universe, and neither can the Christian. Not for us the common dismissal of the Earth as a mere speck in the vastness of space, and mortal men as chance creations of utter insignificance in comparison to the cosmos. Not for us the accusations of arrogance that we err by concentrating so much on ourselves and this little planet, and that we are pumping ourselves up to be something when we are scarcely anything at all. This is a world created with purpose by God, on which He made our first parents in His own image and likeness. This is a world visited by God incarnate. This is the sphere of redeeming grace to be forever the centre of God's purpose. This earth became the setting for the display of greater glory than that seen at the moment the fiat "Let there be light" was uttered, when that Creator Ruler was breathing its air and eating food. As William Cowper says,

> As much, when in the manger laid,
> Almighty ruler of the sky,
> As when the six days' work He made
> Filled all the morning-stars with joy.

He made the stars also surveys planet Earth from this perspective, and Dr Stuart Burgess examines the stars which God also made from an identical geocentricity. Both our world and the heavens seem to sparkle with a new identity as a consequence of this book. Throughout the book there are facts, insights and clear biblical teaching on controversial issues. This makes the book an adventure, enthralling, and very challenging. I suppose that I appreciated it most of all for the strain of doxology that runs like living waters through it all.

Rev Geoff Thomas
Aberystwyth

Notes

1   **Edward J Young,** Studies in Genesis One, Presbyterian and Reformed Publishing Company, p 30, 1964.
2   Ref 1, p 31.
3   **GCh. Aalders,** Genesis, Volume 1, Zondervan, p 53, 1981.

There are over 100 billion stars in our Milky Way Galaxy and there are billions of other galaxies in the Universe. The big Universe raises some equally big questions: What is the origin of the stars? What is the purpose of the stars? Is there life on other planets? The purpose of this book is to present clear biblical answers to these questions.

The question of origins

Chapters 1 and 2 compare the biblical creation account with the Big Bang theory to show the great contrast between the two explanations of origins. Chapter 1 deals with the important questions of starlight and time and the effect of the Fall on the stars.

Chapters 3-6 present the Design Argument by showing how the Universe contains great order, purpose and beauty. The Design Argument is important because it is a biblical argument. In the Bible we read: 'His [God's] invisible attributes are clearly seen, being understood by the things that are made, even His eternal power and Godhead, so that they are without excuse.' (Romans 1:20). From this verse, it is clear that the Design Argument should be understandable to all people whatever their education. I have not given a detailed critique of the Big Bang theory because this would be complicated and would only provide negative evidence against the Big Bang theory rather than positive evidence for the Creator. One of the side-effects of the scientific debate about evolution is that people can sometimes lose sight of the positive nature of the Design Argument. Where relevant I have pointed out basic flaws in the Big Bang theory, but for the most part I have simply argued that chance events cannot explain how the Universe is so finely tuned for the needs of mankind.

Chapters 3 and 4 present traditional arguments of design based on the motion of the stars and the uniqueness of the Earth. Chapter 5 describes evidence not presented before about how the stars are perfectly positioned to shine the right amount of light on the Earth. I hope that this chapter in particular will convince the reader that the Universe really has been designed for mankind. Chapter 6 shows how the outstanding beauty of the Universe represents an important and powerful evidence of design. The most important aspect of the Design Argument is how the Universe reveals God's attributes, so I have devoted a whole chapter to this in Chapter 7. I hope that this chapter will help many readers to stand in awe of God for the way that the stars reveal His great glory, power, wisdom and goodness.

The question of extraterrestrial life

The question of whether there is any extraterrestrial life in the Universe is considered to be one of the most important questions for mankind to address in the twenty-first century. Chapters 8-10 show why man has become so interested in extraterrestrial life and describe some of the current searches for life in space. There is a great need today for people to know what the Bible teaches on this subject. Even though the Bible does not directly address the question of extraterrestrial life, it does give absolutely clear teaching about the purpose of the stars and the importance of the Earth and mankind. Chapter 11 shows how biblical doctrines on creation, redemption and judgement lead to the definite conclusion that there can be no extraterrestrial life.

In Chapter 12 I have given a brief critique of science fiction because this has a major influence on people's belief in extraterrestrial life. Chapter 13 gives an assessment of the rebellion of modern man showing how there are remarkable parallels with the time of Babel. The book finishes on a positive note by describing how the stars remind God's people of some of the wonderful biblical promises concerning God's mercy and grace.

Stuart Burgess
Bristol, 2001

PART ONE
THE QUESTION
OF ORIGINS

The biblical creation account

'By faith we understand that the worlds were framed by the word of God, so that the things which are seen were not made of the things which are visible.' (Hebrews 11:3)

The Bible teaches that the Universe was supernaturally created from nothing by the word of God. Genesis 1 tells us that God chose to create the Earth over the first three days of the creation week and the stars on the fourth day. Since supernatural events are outside of natural laws, there is no reason to doubt that this is exactly the way in which the Universe was created. Since God has given us a detailed account of creation, it is very important for Christians to believe that Genesis 1 is literal. The following sections explain that the order of creation is very encouraging because it shows that the Earth and mankind are right at the centre of God's purposes in the Universe.

1.1 The creation of the Earth and stars

The creation of the Earth and the stars is described in Genesis 1:1-19. A brief commentary on these verses is given in the following sections:

DAY 1 Creation of time, space, Earth and light

'In the beginning, God created the heavens and the Earth. The Earth was without form, and void; and darkness was on the face of the deep. And the Spirit of God was hovering over the face of the waters. Then God said, "Let there be light"; and there was light.' (Genesis 1:1-3)

In the first verse of the Bible, the words 'beginning' and 'heavens' have the meaning of 'time' and 'space'. The reason why 'heavens' refers to just the space of the Universe and not the stars of the Universe is that the stars were made on the fourth day. It is useful to note that there are three types of heaven mentioned in the Bible: the first heaven, the second heaven and the third heaven. The first heaven is the Earth's atmosphere (Genesis 1:8), the second heaven is the space of the entire Universe (Genesis 1:1) and the third heaven is the spiritual heaven (2 Corinthians 12:2). Even though the term 'second heaven' can sometimes include the stars, in Genesis 1:1 it refers only to the space of the Universe.

As well as creating time and space on Day One, God also created the Earth. Reformed Bible commentators such as Henry Morris conclude that the Earth was initially created as a formless lump of matter and that at a later stage on Day One this formless mass was supernaturally formed into a sphere.[1] The reason for this interpretation is that the Bible says that the Earth was initially 'without form and void'. In addition, the Bible teaches that God drew a 'circle on the face of the deep' (Proverbs 8:27). This verse indicates that God formed the spherical shape of the Earth on Day One. It is reasonable to assume that God drew the circle on the face of the deep when the 'Spirit of God was hovering over the face of the waters' (Genesis 1:2). Another reason for concluding that the Earth had a spherical shape by the end of Day One is that the Earth was ready to receive an atmosphere on Day Two. Even though the exact events of Day One are a mystery, we can be certain that the Earth possessed its spherical shape by the end of Day One.

At the end of Day One, the Earth had all of its foundations in place and it had a covering of water. The foundations must have been in place because Genesis 1 does not mention any creative act relating to the foundations of the Earth after Day One. The Earth must have had a covering of water because the water was ready to be separated on Day Two. The fact that the Earth was called 'The Earth' on Day One confirms that the Earth had many of the attributes that made it worthy of being called 'the Earth'.

God also created light on the first day. This light was not produced by natural means of a sun but was supernaturally produced by God. The production of light without a sun raises the question of where the light came from. God may have created beams of light or the light may have come from God Himself. However, the Bible is silent on this matter so either method may have been used. The existence of a morning and evening raises the question of how day and night were produced on the Earth. It is reasonable to assume that the Earth was spinning on its axis in relation to the light source since the Earth would have been spinning in relation to the Sun on the fourth day. At the end of Day One, the Earth would have looked like a water-covered sphere which was slowly rotating and lit up on one side by light.

The first day of creation contains miracles that cannot be comprehended by the human mind. God created the Earth out of nothing by verbal commands. God made light by commanding light to appear. The creation of the Earth and light out of nothing was only possible because of the almighty power of an almighty God.

DAY 2 **Creation of atmosphere and clouds**
'Then God said, "Let there be a firmament in the midst of the waters, and let it divide the waters from the waters." Thus God made the firmament, and divided the waters which were under the firmament from the waters which were above the firmament; and it was so. And God called the firmament Heaven.' (Genesis 1:6-8)

On Day Two there was the creation of a firmament and a separation of the waters into the waters below the firmament and the waters above the firmament. Most Bible commentators conclude that the term 'firmament' here refers to the Earth's atmosphere and that the phrase 'waters which were above the firmament' refers to the water vapour in the upper levels of the atmosphere. The water vapour could have been in the form of clouds as we see them today. However, it is more likely that the water vapour was in the form of an invisible water canopy that probably existed until the time of Noah's flood. The reason for the water-canopy theory is that the Bible speaks of water coming from the ground to water the earth, so there was no need for clouds and rain until after the Flood (Genesis 2:6). Also, the insulating effect of the water canopy can explain why the polar regions of the earth used to have a sub-tropical climate.

Humphreys has recently proposed the idea that the 'waters which were above the firmament' refers to a water canopy around the edge of the

Universe rather than a water canopy around the Earth.[2] However, this interpretation is difficult to defend because the biblical creation account speaks only about the visible world. In his Genesis commentary, John Calvin argues that the waters above the firmament cannot refer to water around the edge of the Universe for the following reasons:

'For, to my mind, this is a certain principle, that nothing is here treated of but the visible form of the world… Whence I conclude, that the waters here meant [the waters above] are such as the rude and unlearned may perceive…Since, therefore, God has created the clouds, and assigned them a region above us, it ought not to be forgotten that they are restrained by the power of God.'[3]

Calvin considered it a 'certain principle' that Genesis 1 refers only to the visible world. In addition, he asserts that terminology in Genesis 1 must be interpreted in a way that ordinary people would understand. From these principles it must be concluded that the waters above the firmament refer to water in the sky and not water around the edge of the Universe. At the end of Day Two, the Earth would have looked like a water-covered sphere with a beautiful blue atmosphere as seen from space.

It is interesting to note that until modern times there was no obvious reason to believe that there was a special atmosphere around the Earth. This is because the Earth's atmosphere is invisible when looking from the surface of the Earth. Only in modern times have observations from space shown that there is a very distinct atmosphere that clings to the Earth. The fact that the book of Genesis, which was written thousands of years ago, highlights the atmosphere as being a major part of creation, shows that the Bible is not based on the ideas of man but that it has been inspired by God.

DAY 3   Creation of land and plants

'Then God said, "Let the waters under the heavens be gathered together into one place, and let the dry land appear"; and it was so. And God called the dry land Earth, and the gathering together of the waters He called Seas. And God saw that it was good. Then God said, "Let the Earth bring forth grass, the herb that yields seed, and the fruit tree that yields fruit according to its kind, whose seed is in itself, on the Earth"; and it was so.' (Genesis 1:9-11)

On Day Three God gathered together the water on the Earth in order to make dry land. The dry land could have been supernaturally spoken into existence out of nothing when the waters were gathered together. However, it is also possible that the land was supernaturally formed from pre-existing material that was created on Day One. As John Byl has explained,[4] it may be that on Day Three there was a separation of water and earth-material in the same way that there was a separation of water on Day Two.

God also created plants supernaturally by direct verbal commands. It is important to note that the Earth was finished before the Sun, Moon and stars were even started. Even the plants were finished on the Earth before God started to work on the stars. The plants were able to survive without the Sun because God supernaturally made light shine from Day One as if there were a Sun in the sky. At the end of Day Three, the Earth would have looked very beautiful from space with its blue seas, blue atmosphere and green land.

DAY 4 Creation of Sun, Moon and stars

'Then God said, "Let there be lights in the firmament of the heavens to divide the day from the night; and let them be for signs and seasons, and for days and years; and let them be for lights in the firmament of the heavens to give light on the Earth"; and it was so. Then God made two great lights: the greater light to rule the day, and the lesser light to rule the night. He made the stars also. God set them in the firmament of the heavens to give light on the Earth, and to rule over the day and over the night, and to divide the light from the darkness. And God saw that it was good. So the evening and the morning were the fourth day.' (Genesis 1:14-19)

These verses teach the astounding fact that God made the stars[5] of the entire Universe in one day. In fact, the Bible also teaches that the stars were created in an instant of time at the verbal command of God (Psalm 33:9). It is an awesome thought that God needed only to speak a word and billions upon billions of stars instantly appeared. The ease with which God spoke the stars into existence is emphasised in the phrase: 'He made the stars also'. Having said that God created the Sun and Moon, Genesis 1 adds the minor detail that God made the stars as well! The reason why the stars are a relatively minor detail is that the Sun and Moon have a greater influence on the Earth than the stars.

The verses also teach the wonderful fact that all the stars of the entire Universe exist in order to 'give light on the Earth'. The purpose of the Sun is to give light on the Earth in the day and the purpose of the Moon is to give light on the Earth at night. The stars also have a purpose of providing nightlights for the Earth. People often look at distant stars and galaxies and ask the question: why are they there? The Bible gives us a direct answer: they are there to light up the Earth, to declare God's glory to mankind and to help mankind by giving signs and seasons and days and years. The fact that God 'set' the stars in their place (Genesis 1:17) demonstrates that God wanted the stars to have a particular position in order to shine light on the Earth in the right way.

To illustrate the Earth-centred purpose of the stars it can be helpful to consider the analogy of the lighting of the stage in a concert hall. A concert hall usually has many lights that are directed onto the stage so that the performers are lit up from different angles. When technicians put the spotlights in the concert hall, they set them in place so that they shine the right amount of light in the right direction. In a similar way, the Earth is centre-stage of the Universe and the stars have been set in place so that they light up the Earth from many different angles with the right brightness.

The fourth day of creation must have been an amazing time when the Earth was lit up with the stars of the entire Universe. This is what the puritan Thomas Watson says about the fourth day in his book, *Body of Divinity*:

'The heavens were bespangled with the Sun, Moon, and stars, that so the world's beauty might be beheld and admired.'[6]

(1.2) The central importance of the Earth in the Universe

One of the most important aspects of the biblical creation account is the central importance of the Earth in the Universe. Even though the Earth is small in comparison to the Universe, the Bible teaches that the Earth has been uniquely prepared for life and is centre-stage of the Universe. The central importance of the Earth can be seen in the way that the Earth was the only part of the physical Universe that was gradually formed. Whereas the Sun, Moon and stars were instantaneously spoken into existence on the fourth day of creation, the Earth was gradually formed over three days. On Day One the Earth was formed into a sphere; on Day Two the waters were separated and on Day Three the dry land was made. The fact that the Earth was formed especially to support life is confirmed in Isaiah where we read: 'For thus says the Lord, who created the heavens, who is God, who formed the Earth and made it, who has established it, who did not create it in vain, who formed it to be inhabited...' (Isaiah 45:18).

There are three other aspects of the biblical creation account which show that the Earth is of particular importance in the Universe. Firstly, the Earth was the first object to be made in the Universe. This order is quite striking because the Earth existed without the Sun for the first three days of creation. Secondly, the Earth received a relatively large amount of time for its creation. The Earth was given three days for its creation, compared to only one day for the rest of the entire Universe. This amount of time is remarkable because the Earth represents an absolutely tiny amount of matter compared to the whole Universe. Thirdly, the Sun, Moon and stars are all said to have the purpose of giving light on the Earth. The fact that the stars were made for the benefit of mankind is also stated in Deuteronomy 4:19 where it is written: 'the Sun, the moon, and the stars... God has given to all the peoples under the whole heaven as a heritage.'

The creation account clearly shows that the Earth was being prepared as a home for mankind. In the construction of a family home, it is normal to work first on the house itself before the garden. This is done even though the house may occupy a relatively small amount of land compared to the garden. The reason for this is that the house is of much more value and importance than the garden. In a similar way, God worked first on the Earth and spent more time on the Earth because it is the home of mankind and therefore the most significant part of the Universe. In his Bible commentary, Matthew Henry makes the following analogy between a house and the Earth:

'The world is a great house, consisting of upper and lower stories, the structure stately and magnificent, uniform and convenient, and every room well and wisely furnished.'[7]

The relatively long length of time given to the creation of the Earth also reflects the greater 'complexity' of the Earth. Someone once said that there is more complexity in a butterfly than there is in the rest of the entire Universe. There is a sense in which this is true. A butterfly contains billions of parts with such intricate design that it may well be more complex than all the stars of the Universe put together. Therefore, it is entirely appropriate that God should spend more time on creating the Earth and its inhabitants than the rest of the Universe. The Earth-centred order of creation is very encouraging because it demonstrates that the Earth is centre-stage of the Universe. People who believe that Genesis 1 is a non-literal account of origins are missing out on this encouragement.

(1.3) The central importance of man in the Universe

Another very encouraging aspect of the biblical creation account is the central importance of mankind. There is an interesting parallel between the Earth and mankind that shows the importance of these two parts of creation. Whereas the Earth was the only part of the physical Universe to be formed, so man was the only creature to be formed (Genesis 2:7). The importance of mankind is also demonstrated in the way that man has been made steward over creation. In Genesis we read: 'Then God said, "Let Us make man in Our image, according to Our likeness; let them have dominion over the fish of the sea, over the birds of the air, and over the cattle, over all the Earth and over every creeping thing that creeps on the Earth."' (Genesis 1:26). The special stewardship status of man is also described in Psalm 8: 'You have made him to have dominion over the works of Your hands; You have put all things under his feet...' (Psalm 8:6-8).

The biblical creation account shows that mankind is precious in the sight of God. John Calvin taught that people should contemplate how Genesis 1 reveals God's fatherly love towards man. In his *Institutes* he says the following:

'But we ought in the very order of things diligently to contemplate God's fatherly love towards mankind, in that he did not create Adam until he had lavished upon the Universe all manner of good things. For if he had put him in an Earth as yet sterile and empty, if he had given him life before light, he would have seemed to provide insufficiently for his welfare. Now when he disposed the movements of the Sun and stars to human uses, filled the Earth, waters, and air with living things, and brought forth an abundance of fruits to suffice as foods, in this assuming the responsibility of a foreseeing and diligent father of the family he shows his wonderful goodness towards us.'[8]

1.4 The 'supernatural' manner of creation

Another important aspect of the biblical creation account is the *supernatural* manner of creation. God did not create the Earth and stars by natural processes. Rather, God supernaturally created the Earth and stars by verbal commands. In addition, the Bible is clear that when God gave verbal commands during the creation week, there was instant obedience to those commands.

The supernatural and instantaneous effect of God's verbal command is seen in the creation of light. When God said: "Let there be light", we immediately read the momentous words 'and there was light'. When God commanded the light to appear, light appeared immediately and exactly how God intended. In the remaining verses of Genesis 1, we read on repeated occasions: 'Then God said, "Let there be...", and it was so'. When God said on the fourth day, "Let there be lights in the firmament of the heaven", we can be sure that the stars were supernaturally and instantly created.

The instantaneous creation of the stars is confirmed in Psalm 33 where we read: 'By the Word of the Lord the heavens were made, and all the host of them by the breath of His mouth ...For He spoke, and it was done; He commanded, and it stood fast.' (Psalm 33:6-9). Notice that after the Psalmist declares 'He commanded', we immediately read the words 'and it stood fast'. This shows that there was an immediate obedience to God's command. When an army General commands his soldiers to stand to attention, he expects the command to be immediately obeyed. Since God has infinitely more power and authority than an army General, it is certain that God's command had an immediate effect and the stars suddenly appeared out of nothing.

The fact that there is instant obedience to God's commands is evident in miracles throughout the Bible. When the centurion asked Jesus to heal his servant, he said to Jesus "… only speak a word, and my servant will be healed." (Matthew 8:8). When Joshua commanded the Sun to stand still in order to make a long day, there is no doubt that the Sun obeyed God and stopped immediately (Joshua 10:12-14). In a similar way, there is no doubt that the stars appeared instantly when God spoke on the fourth day of creation.

(1.5) The creation of a 'mature' Universe

Another very important aspect of the biblical creation account is the creation of a 'mature' and fully functioning Universe that was immediately ready for Adam and Eve to enjoy. At the end of the sixth day of creation, the world contained mature creatures, mature plants and two adult people (Adam and Eve). The creation of a mature Universe is exactly what would be expected when considering the *purpose* of the Universe. Since the purpose of the Universe is to enable God to have fellowship with mankind, it is entirely to be expected that the Universe was ready for mankind in a matter of days rather than billions of years.

To illustrate why a mature creation is consistent with the purpose of the Universe, it can be helpful to consider the analogy of man-made design. In the modern world, human designers often try to produce 'mature' products that are fully functioning when new. When brand-new cars were built thirty years ago, the cars were not fully functioning because the engines had to be run-in at low revs. This meant that the owner of a new car had the annoyance of driving slowly for the first 1,000 miles. However, modern car designers have learnt special techniques to make sure that an engine is fully functioning from the beginning of its use. Customers who now buy a brand-new car can drive the car at full speed as soon as they start driving the car. Given that human designers strive to produce artefacts that are fully functioning in as short a time as possible, there is every reason to believe that an infinitely powerful God produced a fully functioning Universe in a very short period of time.

God was able to create a mature and fully functioning Universe because

He is not constrained by natural laws. When God created plants, He super-naturally created roots in the ground and he supernaturally created soil with all the right nutrients. The creation of a mature Universe means that the Universe must be thousands and not billions of years old. If there are no gaps in Bible genealogies, then the age of the Universe can be calculated to be approximately six thousand years old. Some Bible scholars believe that there are gaps in the genealogies and, therefore, the Universe could be older than six thousand years by a few thousand years.

Secular scientists often claim that they have proved that the Universe is billions of years old. However, one of the inevitable consequences of a mature creation is that it has the 'appearance' of age. Flowers, trees, animals, Adam, Eve and stars would have had the appearance of age even during the creation week. When secular scientists argue that the Universe is very old, they are making an assumption that there has been no super-natural creation event. However, Genesis 1 tells us that there *has been* a supernatural creation and, therefore, secular scientists are wrong in their basic assumptions. The effect of supernatural creation can be illustrated with the example of the first recorded miracle of the Lord Jesus. When Jesus turned water into wine, the wine was said to be of the highest quality. Any secular scientist who had inspected that wine would certainly have concluded from the physical evidence that the wine was very old, even though it was actually brand new.

One conclusion that can be drawn is that it is not possible to physically measure age from anything that has been supernaturally created such as stars. A second conclusion is that secular scientists will always see the Universe in a very different way to Christians because of their opposing philosophical views.

(1.6) Starlight in a young Universe

Starlight takes a long time to travel from the stars to the Earth. Even in the case of the closest star it takes about four years for the light to reach the Earth. In the case of the most distant stars it takes billions of years to reach the Earth. If God had made the stars on the fourth day of creation and then had let their light travel to Earth at what we now know as the speed of light, then it would have taken four years before the first star was seen by Adam and Eve. However, there are several reasons for concluding that all the stars were visible on the day that they were made. One reason is that the creation was declared 'good' at the end of Day Four. A second reason is that we do not see stars suddenly 'switching on' now as their starlight reaches the Earth. A third reason is that we know that some of the stars we see are billions of light-years away.

On Day Four of creation, God clearly did something special in order to bring starlight to the Earth so quickly. Because of the supernatural nature of the creation week it is not possible to know for sure how God produced a mature Universe. However, creationists have come up with different possible explanations that show that it was certainly feasible for God to bring distant starlight to the Earth on Day Four of creation. The following sections give a summary of the main theories of distant starlight. In addition, a new and very simple explanation is presented.

❶ Created-in-transit (mature creation)

The 'created-in-transit' theory proposes that God created beams of light *en route* between the stars and the Earth at the same instant that the stars were created.[9] The created-in-transit theory is sometimes referred to as a 'mature creation' theory because it proposes that the Universe had an apparent history in an instant of time. The created-in-transit theory is a very straightforward answer to the question of starlight but an objection has been raised against this explanation on the grounds that starlight would not reflect what has actually happened to the stars. In other words, when we see events such as supernovae in distant stars, the created-in-transit theory proposes that these events did not actually happen to the stars but that what we see simply represents information that God has put into the beams of light. Despite this objection, the created-in-transit theory is consistent with the biblical creation account and the theory has been supported by several leading creationist authors.[9,10,11]

❶ Speed-of-light decay

In order to explain how starlight can reflect what has actually happened to the stars, the speed-of-light decay theory has been proposed as an alternative theory to the created-in-transit theory. The 'speed-of-light decay' theory proposes that the speed of light started off at infinite speed when the stars were created and then gradually decreased according to a natural decay law.[12] In addition to a decay in the speed of light, there would have been a decay in the rate of other physical processes such as radioactive decay. The speed-of-light decay theory provides a straightforward solution to the starlight question. In addition, it has the benefit that it can give a simple explanation to the apparent dates given by radiometric dating of rocks in the Earth. However, an objection has been raised against this theory that there is not yet convincing proof that the speed of light has gradually decreased over time. For example, the speed of light is now known to be constant in the present age and past measurements appear to be too unreliable to draw firm conclusions about possible changes in the past. Despite this objection, it is not possible to disprove the idea of a decay in the speed of light and it is possible that God did use this method.

ⅲ Young-Earth relativistic cosmology

The young-Earth relativistic cosmology theory has also been proposed as an alternative theory to the created-in-transit theory. The 'relativistic cosmology' theory has been described recently in the book *Starlight and Time*.[13] There are two main aspects to the theory. One aspect is that God speeded up the processes of stars relative to the Earth on the fourth day of creation so that billions of years worth of physical processes took place in the distant cosmos including the travelling of starlight from all the stars to the Earth. The second aspect of the theory is that God caused the speeding up to take place primarily by *natural* processes. At first it might appear impossible that natural processes could create billions of years of time during one Earth day. However, the relativistic cosmology theory proposes that God used complex phenomena recently suggested by modern theoretical physics such as a 'white hole', 'relativistic time dilation' and 'expansion of space' in order to create billions of years of time for the stars on Day Four. The theory also proposes that the stars formed from gas clouds over billions of years (in their time frame) in a process similar to that proposed in the secular Big Bang theory.

The first aspect of the relativistic cosmology theory that 'billions of years worth of physical processes took place in the distant cosmos' on the fourth day of creation is a good proposal because it solves the starlight question. In fact, in the next section I will explain that I think that a speeding up of the stars did indeed take place. However, there is a crucial question: did God speed up the stars supernaturally or did God speed up the stars by natural processes in natural timeframes? As described earlier, the Bible clearly reveals that creation was a supernatural event and therefore science cannot be used to explain how the Universe came into being. Therefore, it must be concluded that if God speeded up the stars on the fourth day of creation, then this must have been done supernaturally. There is currently much debate about the scientific validity of the young-Earth relativistic cosmology theory. However, I believe that the debate is purely academic because even if the relativistic cosmology theory were found to be a scientifically valid theory, God would not have used this method because it is based on natural processes.

▶ NEW EXPLANATION OF STARLIGHT

ⓥ Speeded-up stars

The speeded-up stars theory proposes that just after creating the stars, God temporarily speeded up the physical processes of the Universe in order to bring starlight from all the stars immediately to the Earth. The speeded-up stars theory involves the following course of events. Firstly, God supernaturally and instantaneously created the stars on the fourth day of creation. (At the initial point of creation, the Universe would have been smaller than it is now with distant galaxies being much closer than they are now and with nearby galaxies being slightly closer than they are now.) Just after creating the stars, God supernaturally made all the processes of stars occur at near infinite speed so that the stars went through a 'long history of events' in an instant of time. (The further away a star is from the Earth, the more the star processes were speeded up). For example, God made the Universe expand at a rate which was up to billions of times faster than it now expands (although the stars did not experience the forces produced by these accelerated speeds because of the supernatural nature of the speeding up). Also, God made the stars emit light at a rate which was up to billions of times faster than they now emit light and He made their starlight travel up to billions of times faster than it now travels.

The result of this speeding up of the processes in the stars was that the starlight from all the stars in the Universe reached the Earth in a just a brief moment and the starlight reflected events that had actually taken place in the stars. For example, when we observe a distant galaxy receding from the Earth we are observing a movement that has actually happened. After bringing starlight to the Earth, God made all the star processes reduce in speed to what we now call 'normal' speeds. For example, the speed of starlight from distant stars was suddenly reduced to what we now know as the speed of light and the rate of expansion of the Universe was suddenly reduced to what we now know as the normal rate of expansion.

Since God is the Creator and Sustainer of natural laws, it would have been easy for Him to temporarily speed up the Universe in this way. Also, given that God wanted to make a mature Universe in an instant of time, it is entirely consistent with His character that He should have overruled the now normal laws of physics to bring starlight to the Earth on Day Four of creation.

The speeded-up stars theory has very strong scriptural support because the Bible teaches that God stretched out the heavens like a curtain (Psalm 104:2). In the same way that it takes only a moment to stretch out a curtain, so it took God only a moment to stretch out the Universe (including starlight), following the supernatural creation of the stars. The Bible also teaches that God will one day roll up the Universe like a scroll (Isaiah 34:3). Since the Universe will be rolled up in moment at some point in the future, it makes sense that the Universe was stretched out in a moment on the fourth day of creation.

If God has indeed speeded up the stars as described above, then when we look at distant stars we are seeing events that took place in an instant of time. However, it looks as if the events in these distant stars have taken place at a normal rate. Some people might object to the idea that when we see distant stars we are seeing events that happened in an instant of time. However, it should be taken into account that all starlight theories involve billions of years of events occurring in a very short period of time. In addition, it should be remembered that the creation week was full of supernatural events and therefore outside of natural laws.

An analogy can be made between the speeding up of stars and the winding forward of a videotape. When a videotape is fast-forwarded, the television screen emits speeded-up images in a few seconds that would normally take several minutes to play. If it were possible to suddenly slow down the speed at which these compressed images are travelling through the air (just before they reach the viewer), then the viewer would see several minutes of images and these images would appear to take place at the right speed. In a similar way, God could have 'fast-forwarded' the stars and galaxies until their starlight reached the Earth and then supernaturally slowed down all the processes of stars to 'normal' speeds. In addition to a temporary speeding up of the speed of light, there could also have been a temporary speeding up of other physical processes such as radioactive decay.

The speeded-up stars theory is arguably the best starlight theory because it is consistent with the instantaneous creation of the stars and because it produces a mature Universe in an instant of time where starlight reflects events which have actually happened to the stars. However, it is important to note that we can never be sure exactly how God created a mature Universe. One thing that is certain is that God would have had no difficulty whatsoever in creating a mature Universe. As a final point, it should be remembered that the most important aspect of the stars is not how distant starlight reached the Earth on Day Four of creation. The most important aspect of the stars is how they reveal God's glory, power, wisdom and goodness. These aspects will be covered in Chapters 3-7.

(1.7) The effect of the Fall

The Bible teaches that God put a curse on the whole of creation following the disobedience of Adam and Eve in the Garden of Eden (Genesis 3:17-19 and Romans 8:20-22). We do not know exactly when the Fall took place, but most Bible commentators believe that it was very soon after the end of the creation week. Since the Universe is in a fallen state, it is probable that we do not see the stars exactly as they appeared before the Fall. We cannot know for certain how the stars appeared before the Fall, but there are some conclusions that we can make:

ⓘ The constellations were the same before the Fall

It is reasonable to assume that the layout of the stars and their constellations was the same before the Fall. The reason for this is that the purpose of the curse was to put the Universe into a fallen state and not to make everything look completely different. For example, star constellations such as Orion would doubtless have existed on the fourth day of creation.

ⓘ There was probably no decay of stars before the Fall

All stars now decay and die out as they run out of fuel and shrink or explode into supernovae. This raises the important question of whether stars were in a state of decay before the Fall. Morris argues that there was no decay before the Fall:

'…the Bible teaches that, originally, there was no disorder, no decay, no ageing process, no suffering, and above all, no death, in the world when the creation was completed. All was 'very good''![14]

The principle that there was no decay before the Fall seems to have strong scriptural support. For example, the current decay of the stars is described in Hebrews 1:10-11, where we read that the stars will 'perish' and 'grow old like a garment'. The fact that Hebrews 1 tells us that the stars will grow old, strongly indicates that the stars were not growing old before the Fall. Also, since the original creation was intended to last for eternity, it is reasonable to assume that the stars were designed to last for eternity. Indeed, the eternal nature of the original stars is referred to in Psalm 148:6. Some people object to the idea of an eternal star on the grounds that the concept is now physically impossible. However, there are many things that we cannot explain about the original paradise, so we cannot rule out eternal stars on the grounds that we cannot explain how they functioned.

Some authors have argued that there must have been decay in the Universe before the Fall because there must have been physical effects such as friction. However, friction itself does not cause decay. In our present world, friction does of course lead to *secondary* decay effects such as wear and heat. However, there is no reason to assume that friction caused the same secondary effects before the Fall. Indeed, it would be most logical to assume that things were not subject to wear before the Fall because life was eternal.

Whilst there are strong biblical arguments for concluding that the stars did not decay before the Fall, the arguments are not absolutely conclusive and therefore it is necessary to exercise caution. The best conclusion to draw is that the stars were 'probably' not in a state of decay before the Fall.

(iii) The original starlight was probably replaced at the time of the Fall

If God did change the stars into decaying stars at the time of the Fall, then He would have removed the original starlight from the perfect stars and replaced it with light from the fallen stars so that we now see the stars in a fallen state. The removal of the original starlight might at first seem strange. However, it must be remembered that great changes occurred to the whole of creation at the time of the Fall. For example, some plants were given thorns and some creatures were given sharp claws and teeth. Such changes involved the replacement of something good with something fallen. Therefore, it is reasonable to believe that the original starlight was probably changed at the time of the Fall.

(iv) The fallen stars still show evidence of order and beauty

Even though the stars are now in a state of decay, they still contain great order and beauty and they still declare the glory of God. It is even the case that aspects of decay such as supernovae and planetary nebulae can appear very beautiful even though they probably appeared only as a result of God's curse on creation at the time of the Fall. Some people may object to the idea that something as beautiful as a supernova could have existed only after the Fall. However, there are many parts of creation which are beautiful despite having an origin which relates to the Fall. For example, thorns, thistles and grey hairs can be considered to be beautiful even though they only exist because of the Fall. Also, many people consider predators to be beautiful even though predators owe much of their design to the Fall.

(1.8) Ten reasons why Genesis 1 is literal

Many teachers in theological seminaries teach that Genesis 1 is just poetic language and should not be taken literally. The reason behind this stance is that there is an assumption that secular scientific theories must be right. Since the Big Bang theory involves a different order and timing of creation to the account given in Genesis 1, liberal theologians conclude that Genesis 1 must be poetic. The assumption that secular science must be right is, of course, an incorrect assumption. Also, there are at least ten reasons why Genesis 1 must be understood as a literal account of origins:

❶ The original Hebrew indicates a literal account

Hebrew scholars agree that the most obvious translation of Genesis 1 is that the days are literal 24-hour days. The Hebrew word found in Genesis 1 is the word 'yom' and this normally refers to a 24-hour day. The fact that Genesis 1 refers to 'mornings' and 'evenings' reinforces the conclusion that the creation days were literal.

❷ The book of Exodus supports a six-day creation

In the book of Exodus we read: 'For in six days the Lord made the heavens and the Earth' (Exodus 20:11). In order to reinforce the importance of a day of rest at the end of a working week, God refers to the fact that He took six days and not six time periods to create the world. The fact that God uses the creation week to reinforce the importance of the Sabbath day shows that the creation week was a literal week.

❸ The Lord Jesus referred to a recent creation

In the Gospel of Mark we read: '...from the beginning of the creation, God made them male and female' (Mark 10:6). In this verse, Jesus speaks out against divorce and He refers to the fact that God made male and female to exist from the beginning of creation. According to the Big Bang theory, people have existed only relatively recently in history and there were billions of years when no one existed. In contrast, the biblical creation account teaches that people have existed from the sixth day of creation, i.e. people have existed from virtually the beginning of the existence of the Universe. Therefore, this verse in Mark 10 shows that Jesus fully believed that the biblical creation account was literal. In the Gospel of Luke we also read: '...the blood of all the prophets which was shed from the foundation of the world' (Luke 11:50). This verse teaches that the blood of the prophets began to be shed very shortly after the world was created. These words of the Lord Jesus again show that the creation week must be interpreted as a literal week.

ⓘⓥ The Apostle Peter referred to a recent creation

In the book of Acts we read: '...God has spoken by the mouth of all His holy prophets since the world began' (Acts 3:21). This verse teaches that the prophets started speaking shortly after the creation of the world. These words of the Apostle Peter again show that the creation week must be interpreted as a literal week.

ⓥ The Apostle Paul referred to a recent creation

In the book of Romans we read: 'For since the creation of the world His invisible attributes are clearly seen...' (Romans 1:20). This verse clearly implies that there have been people from the beginning of creation who have seen God's attributes. God's attributes would have been seen by Adam and Eve on the very day that the creation was finished. These words of the Apostle Paul again show that the creation week must be interpreted as a literal week.

ⓥⓘ The new heavens and new Earth will not be made by Big Bang evolution

This present Universe will one day be dissolved and new heavens and a new Earth will be created in a supernatural way (Isaiah 65:17). It is inconceivable that the new heavens and new Earth will be evolved over billions of years. In a similar way, we can be confident that the present Universe has not evolved.

ⓥⓘⓘ God was intimately involved in creation

The Bible describes God as being a 'master craftsman' who was intimately involved in every detail of creation. In the book of Job we read that God determined the measurements of the foundations of the Earth and that He stretched a line upon it (Job 38:5). In the book of Proverbs we read '...when He drew a circle on the face of the deep...When He marked out the foundations of the Earth, then I was beside Him as a master craftsman'[15] (Proverbs 8:27-30). The description of God as a great craftsman measuring out the dimensions of the foundations of the Earth supports the conclusion that God did not use evolution because a craftsman carries out instantaneous and deliberate actions whereas evolution involves a long random process.

⑧ Use of poetry does not prevent a literal account

Some liberal theologians try to argue that God's aim was to write a poetic account of creation and therefore the account should not be taken literally. However, since God is infinitely wise, He can easily write beautiful poetry that is based on a literal account. Many of the psalms are written in beautiful poetry at the same time as containing profound truth. God does not need to change the account of creation in order to write beautiful poetry. Some liberal theologians argue that the parallelism between Days One to Three and Days Four to Six supports a non-literal interpretation. On Day One God created light, and on Day Four God created the stars. On Day Two God created the seas and sky, and on Day Five God created the fish and birds. On Day Three God created the land and plants, and on Day Six God created the land creatures. However, just because there is parallelism between Days One to Three and Days Four to Six, this does not provide evidence against Genesis 1 being literal. Since God created the Universe in a supernatural way, He was free to create the Universe in any order He wanted. That God chose an elegant order with parallelism between Days One to Three and Four to Six is entirely consistent with God's infinite wisdom.

⑨ A literal account has been believed for four millennia

For at least four millennia, the vast majority of theologians have assumed that the creation account is a literal account. The fact that so many people over such a long period of time have believed Genesis 1 to be literal provides strong evidence that God meant the creation account to be interpreted in this way. All the great Bible commentators of the puritan times assumed it was a literal account. It is only in modern times that significant numbers of theologians have denied the literal interpretation so that they do not have to disagree with the Big Bang theory.

⊗ The earliest people could understand a literal account

Another argument that liberal theologians use for Genesis 1 being non-literal is that God needed to use simple terms for the first generations of people on the Earth. This argument is based on the assumption that the first humans were primitive in understanding. However, there are strong arguments for believing that the first people on the Earth were very intelligent. The first people on the Earth lived much longer than people do today with life spans of several centuries. With such long lives, people were able to accumulate much knowledge and also pass on this knowledge to their children. In addition, the first people were almost certainly not so affected by genetic disorders as people today. The intelligence of early people was such that God did not need to write a simplified account of origins.

(1.9) Consistency between scientific principles and Genesis 1

There is a popular misconception that science has shown that miracles do not happen and cannot happen. This is why modern scientists argue that the biblical creation account is not a valid theory of origins. It is also why the biblical creation account is not taught as a possible account of origins in physics and biology books. However, science has not proved that miracles do not happen. Science simply shows how things work when miracles are not in operation. One of the useful aspects of scientific understanding is that it actually helps to identify when a miracle has taken place.

The origin of the Universe is a prime example of where natural processes cannot possibly account for what has happened. This is because the creation of the Universe involved physical matter appearing from nothing. Therefore, any theory of origins must take into account that the ultimate origin of the Universe involved a miraculous act. The Bible clearly teaches that the creation of the initial space, time and matter was a miracle. The Bible says that '...the things which are seen were not made of the things which are visible' (Hebrews 11:3). Since the Bible describes a miraculous act behind the creation of the first matter, the biblical creation account is consistent with scientific principles.

The consistency between the Bible and scientific principles is also demonstrated by the fact that many scientists, past and present, have had no difficulty in accepting the supernatural creation account. For example, great scientists like Lord Kelvin, Clerk Maxwell and Isaac Newton had a very firm belief in a Creator God. Recently, there has been the publication of a book: *In Six Days: Why 50 Scientists Believe*.[16] This book contains contributions from 50 scientists with at least a PhD qualification. All 50 scientists believe that Genesis 1 is a literal account of creation in six 24-hour days.

(1.10) Our response to the creation account

The most important response we can make to Genesis 1 is to believe that it is a literal account of origins. God has been very good towards mankind in giving such a detailed account of creation. He has also been very good in providentially preserving the words of the Bible over many centuries. The fact that God has given mankind the creation account means that it must be important for spiritual health. Therefore, it is important to believe and meditate upon the teaching of Genesis 1.

Another response that we can make to Genesis 1 is to rejoice in what it says. To be able to read an account of origins written by the Creator Himself is a great privilege and one that can be greatly enjoyed. To read a blow by blow account of the creation of the Universe is more thrilling than the most dramatic film or novel could ever be. It is sad that so many people dismiss Genesis 1 as non-literal poetry when it is such an exciting account of what actually happened. It is interesting that children often have no difficulty with Genesis 1. This is not because children have simple minds but because they have not been indoctrinated with the ideas of this world. In Job 38:7 we read how the morning stars (i.e. angels) sang for joy during the creation week. When we read the creation account, we too can have great joy in our hearts.

It is good to believe and to rejoice in Genesis 1, but even this is not enough. When we read of God's supernatural and instantaneous method of creation, we must stand in awe of Him. The ease with which God spoke the Universe into existence is illustrated by the words used in Genesis 1:16 where it is written: 'He made the stars also'. It is amazing how such few words are used to describe such a profound act. This little phrase refers to God speaking into existence billions of galaxies, every single one of which contains the order of a billion stars. We can hardly imagine the matter and energy in one star, let alone a galaxy of stars or a Universe of stars. When we consider God speaking the vast Universe of stars into existence, we can do nothing but stand in awe of Him.

Notes on Chapter 1

1   **Morris, H,** *The Genesis Record,* Baker Books, Genesis 1:1, pp 51-52, 1976.
2   **Humphreys, R,** *Starlight and Time,* Master Books, Green Forest, p 35, 1994.
3   **Calvin, J,** *Genesis,* Banner of Truth Trust, p 79, 1965.
4   **Byl, J,** *God and Cosmos,* Banner of Truth, p 161, 2001.
5   The term 'lights' includes all the stars, planets, gas clouds and everything else that exists in space. Planets can be considered stars since they shine light on the Earth by virtue of reflecting the Sun's rays.
6   **Watson, T,** *A body of divinity* (1692), The Banner of Truth Trust, Chapter 13 The Creation, p 114, 1965.
7   **Henry, M,** *Bible commentary,* Mac Donald, Genesis 1:1, p 2.
8   **Calvin, J,** *Institutes of the Christian Religion 1,* Westminster, Chapter 14, pp 161-162.
9   Ref 1, p 66.
10 **DeYoung, DB,** *Astronomy and the Bible,* Baker, Grand Rapids, Second Edition, pp 89-90, 2000.
11 Ref 2, p 194.
12 **Setterfield, B,** *Carbon 14 Dating, tree ring dating and speed of light decay,* CENTJ, v2, pp 169-188, 1986.
13 Ref 2.
14 **Morris, H,** *The Twilight of Evolution,* Philadelphia: Presbyterian and Reformed, 1963, p 37.
15 The NKJV uses the term master craftsman but the Authorised Version does not.
16 **Ashton, J,** (Editor) *In Six Days – Why 50 Scientists Believe,* New Holland, 1999.

The Big Bang theory

'I am the Lord, who makes all things, who stretches out the heavens all alone, who spreads abroad the Earth by myself; who frustrates the signs of the babblers, and drives diviners mad; who turns wise men backward, and makes their knowledge foolishness' (Isaiah 44:24-25).

Since supernatural events are outside of natural laws, science can tell us nothing about how the Universe came into being. Despite this fundamental fact, many scientists claim that the Big Bang theory can fully explain how the Universe came into being without any reference to a Creator. The Big Bang theory is now taught as a 'fact' of science in schools, universities and the media. However, the Big Bang theory is not a reflection of scientific evidence. Rather, it is a reflection of the desire of many secular scientists to produce an account of origins that does not require belief in a Creator God. Over the last two centuries, there has been a gradual shift from a scientific community that largely believed in the God of the Bible to a scientific community that is largely atheistic.

In the present age we are witnessing God's judgement on modern science as described in the book of Isaiah. Some areas of modern science, such as Big Bang cosmology, are being turned backwards with many theories becoming foolish in the extreme.

2.1 The Big Bang theory

According to the Big Bang theory, everything we see in the Universe today has evolved out of a random explosion of matter. Secular scientists sometimes refer to the theoretical process of star formation as 'stellar evolution'. People who believe in the Big Bang theory will be referred to as evolutionists for the remainder of this book. The use of the term 'evolutionist' is not meant to imply that such people also believe in biological evolution. A typical summary of the Big Bang theory up to the point of the evolution of galaxies is given in the following quotation, taken from the *Greenwich Guide to Stars, Galaxies and Nebulae*:

'This is how the Universe started about 15 billion years ago… everything in the Universe was jam-packed together in one place as a super dense blob… the Universe suddenly came into existence all at one place with an almighty bang, incomparably more powerful than anything that has ever happened since, which flung the material far out into space and was directly responsible for the expansion of the Universe which is still going on…By the time the Universe was one ten-thousandth of a second old, quarks and mesons forged in the inferno, the temperature had dropped to a million million K and the density was down to 10 million million times that of lead…As the Big Bang continued, the Universe spread out and its temperature and density dropped, allowing sub-atomic particles to form. By the time 10 seconds had elapsed, many sub-atomic particles were welded together to form the nuclei of atoms… Radiation – energy in the form of heat and light – continued to dominate for the next million years, by which time the temperature had dropped to below 10,000K…After the first million years had elapsed, the Universe was a huge cloud of uniform, thin gas rather hotter than the surface of the Sun…over many millions of years, the Universe became divided up into innumerable blobs of gas which would eventually become clusters of galaxies. At the same time, the Universe continued to expand, increasing the distance between the blobs…Within the blobs, the same process was going on, on a smaller scale, with each one breaking up into millions of much smaller blobs which would form into stars. When a galaxy was still largely composed of gas, collisions between particles would be quite frequent, and this would help the process of knocking the galaxy into its final shape.'[1]

The words 'flung' and 'collisions' in the quotation above show that evolutionists believe that everything in the Universe has originated by naturalistic processes and chance. Many cosmologists do not like the Big Bang theory being referred to as an explosion of matter, arguing that it is really an 'expansion of space and matter'. However, the use of the terms 'inferno' and 'almighty bang' in the quotation above show that the description of explosion is actually quite appropriate. The reason why cosmologists prefer the term expansion is that this term sounds less random than the term explosion. However, no amount of playing with terminology can change the fact that the Big Bang theory is based on random processes.

A typical summary of the theory of the evolution of the Solar System is given in the following quotations from the *Greenwich Guide to Stars, Galaxies and Nebulae* and the *Greenwich Guide to The Planets*:

'...the Sun is not one of the stars that first started to condense when the Universe was still young, and this makes an important difference to its composition. The very first stars were composed of only the lightest elements: mostly hydrogen, some helium...The gas cloud from which our Sun formed had been enriched with heavier elements [carbon, oxygen, nitrogen, iron etc], formed in an earlier generation of stars and then dispersed through the galaxy when these stars exploded...'[2]

'If we were to have visited the region of the Solar System some 4600 million years ago, we would have found a gently rotating cloud of gas and dust, mostly made up of hydrogen but also containing a small proportion of other elements. This is the cloud from which the Sun and planets condensed... our cloud broke up into a large number of blobs which moved around, bumping into one another and sometimes breaking up and sometimes coalescing... The disc of material has now become a large number of lumps up to 1,000 km across, all orbiting the Sun in the same direction. They will continue to collide with one another to form a few big lumps and these will sweep up most of the smaller ones...Most of this process, from gas cloud to Sun and planets, took place in just a few million years... Since then, the planets have been steadily cooling.'[3]

One of the most important things to notice in the quotations is that there is no mention of a Creator God. The absence of a Creator God from descriptions of the Big Bang theory shows that it really is an atheistic theory. In addition, these descriptions of the Big Bang theory tacitly promote atheism, even though they do not explicitly state a belief in atheism.

Also notice from the quotations how the Big Bang theory proposes that the Solar System has evolved from material that has come from exploding stars. Therefore, according to the Big Bang theory, there have been at least two big explosions in the formation of the Earth. The belief that the Earth has formed from the remnants of a supernova explains why many astronomy books teach that human beings are 'children of the stars'. For example, one popular book on astronomy says the following:

'We are children of the stars, our planet and all things on it forming through the collecting together of elements produced during supernova explosions aeons ago. Perhaps, therefore, part of the wonder of looking up into the night sky is the thought that we are looking back at our roots.'[4]

(2.2) The unimportance of the Earth in the Big Bang theory

Biblical teaching about the central importance of the Earth is totally rejected by secular astronomers. Modern books on astronomy refer to the Earth as just an ordinary planet that orbits an ordinary star in an ordinary galaxy.[5,6,7] Evolutionists also believe that mankind is totally unimportant on the scale of the Universe. The insignificance of the Earth and man in the Big Bang theory is illustrated in the following quotation from a popular writer on atheism, PW Atkins:

'Man is not intrinsically significant…Think of the Universe as a puff of dust about 1 metre in diameter. Every dust grain is a galaxy. We live near a rather ordinary star which is a member of a rather ordinary galaxy somewhere insignificant in the puff of dust.'[8]

The unimportance of the Earth in the Big Bang theory makes a great contrast with the biblical creation account which teaches that the Earth is right at the centre of God's purposes in the Universe. Atheists look at the billions of stars in the Universe and conclude that the Earth is utterly insignificant. They reason that if God had made the stars for the Earth, then He would have created only a few thousand stars because that is all that is needed to give adequate light at night and to produce signs and seasons. But this reasoning is wrong because it assumes that God would have done the minimum amount of work necessary to satisfy the needs of mankind. In reality, it is entirely consistent with God's character to make trillions of stars where just a few thousand would have sufficed. God has given bountiful supplies of stars because of His great fatherly love for mankind. In addition, the vast number of stars also helps to reveal the attributes of God. It is tragic how modern science uses the number of stars to argue for atheism, when the great number of stars actually helps us to know that there is a God!

2.3 The 'naturalistic' character of the Big Bang theory

One of the most important aspects of the Big Bang theory is that it is an entirely 'naturalistic' theory. The Big Bang theory involves the evolution of space and matter by natural processes and the forming of stars and planets by natural means. The naturalistic character of the Big Bang theory makes it diametrically opposed to the biblical creation account. Whereas Genesis 1 records nothing but supernatural acts of creation by a Creator God, the Big Bang theory contains nothing but natural processes where God is not needed. The naturalistic character of the Big Bang theory should not be surprising because the whole purpose of the Big Bang theory is to explain the origin of the Universe without reference to God.

The ambition of many modern scientists to remove God from origins as much as possible is illustrated in the following quotation from PW Atkins:

'My aim is to argue that the Universe can come into existence without intervention, and that there is no need to invoke the idea of a Supreme Being ... Our task should now be clear... We have to embark upon the track of the absolute zero of intervention... The only faith we need for the journey is the belief that everything can be understood and, ultimately, that there is nothing to explain... I shall try to show that most of the concepts that at first sight seem crucial to our understanding of the workings of the world can be allowed to evaporate. When they have gone they will leave behind what we should truly and usefully consider: that is, virtually nothing.'[9]

Notice in this quotation the words 'My aim', 'Our task' and 'faith we need'. These words illustrate the fact that atheism requires just as much faith as any religious viewpoint. The quotation also shows that the ultimate goal of the Big Bang theory is to convince people that they do not need to believe in a Creator God. There is a strong argument for making a connection between the huge growth in atheism in the last one hundred years and the teaching of the Big Bang theory and the theory of biological evolution in schools and universities. Even if the Big Bang theory does not produce atheism, the theory does little to inspire people to believe in a great God.

(2.4) Arguments against the Big Bang theory

The media and education system claim that there is strong evidence to support the Big Bang theory. For example, they teach that the observed expansion of the Universe is evidence that the stars and galaxies must have come from an explosion of dense matter in the distant past. They also teach that the cosmic background radiation is evidence of an after-glow of a Big Bang explosion. Despite these claims, there are very strong philosophical and technical arguments against the Big Bang theory.

❶ Philosophical arguments against the Big Bang theory

One philosophical problem with the Big Bang theory is that it cannot explain where the first matter came from. In fact, there can never be a satis-factory scientific explanation to this problem because science is based on the fact that something cannot be created from nothing in a natural process. A second philosophical problem with the Big Bang theory is that it cannot explain why the Universe started at a particular time. If all the matter of the Universe was once condensed into a tiny blob that was smaller than a pinhead, then the most logical outcome is that it should always have stayed in the form of a tiny blob. In order to illustrate these philosophical problems, someone once explained the Big Bang theory in the following way: 'In the beginning there was nothing, then it exploded!'.

❷ Technical arguments against the Big Bang theory

One of the main technical arguments against the Big Bang theory is the lack of evidence for star formation. According to the Big Bang theory, stars form when gas clouds contract into a ball of hot matter. However, there is very little direct evidence of this happening. In contrast, there is a great deal of direct evidence that many stars are decaying and disappearing. For example, novae and supernovae represent direct evidence for the death of stars. Even if there are some stars forming from gas clouds, the current evidence would still strongly indicate that there are many more stars dying than being born. Therefore, the overall trend is for a decaying Universe and not a Universe where stars form by natural processes.

Whilst it can be helpful to know that there are technical problems with the Big Bang theory, it is important to understand that there are limitations to these arguments. One limitation is that the technical evidences against the Big Bang theory are often very complicated and only understandable to experts in Big Bang cosmology. A second limitation with technical arguments is that the Big Bang theory is constantly changing. Every time a technical flaw is discovered in the Big Bang theory, the theory is quickly modified to overcome the criticism. Also, mathematics is so flexible and people are so ingenious that there is always likely to be an answer to any technical criticism made against the Big Bang theory.

2.5 The Design Argument

The Universe does not reveal evidence of natural processes. Rather, the Universe contains great order and beauty that provides evidence of supremely intelligent design. For example, in Chapter 3 it will be shown that the expansion of the Universe (and the accompanying galactic red-shift) probably exists in order to give stability to the Universe. Galactic red-shift may also exist in order to give beauty to the Universe. Therefore, there is every reason to believe that God created mature stars on Day Four and that the stars were given motions at the time of their creation so that the Universe would be instantly an expanding Universe. The fact that there is a logical reason why God should make the Universe expand means that there is no reason to see the expansion of the Universe as an evidence of a Big Bang.

There may well also be a logical reason for cosmic background radiation. However, the cosmic background radiation is such a minor detail in the Universe that it is difficult to see why this should be considered as serious evidence for a Big Bang anyway. Whatever the temperature of deep space had been found to be at the present time, the evolutionist was always going to say that this was the afterglow of a Big Bang. Even if the temperature of the universe had been found to be zero, the Big Bang model would have been adjusted to predict a zero temperature at this point in time! Of course, the evolutionist will always claim that the cosmic background radiation is a very significant piece of evidence for the Big Bang theory. However, this just shows how the evolutionist has to clutch at straws.

One way of describing evidences of design is to identify hallmarks of an intelligent designer. An intelligent designer is not restricted by step by step change and can produce levels of order and beauty that cannot be produced by evolution. In another book *Hallmarks of Design*,[10] I describe six hallmarks of design that can only be produced by an intelligent designer: irreducible mechanisms; complete optimum design; added beauty; extreme similarity; extreme diversity; and man-centred features. In Chapters 3-6 of this book it will be shown that these hallmarks of design are seen throughout the Universe.

There are several reasons why the design argument is the most important argument for a Creator. One reason is that the design argument is a biblical argument which gives people no excuse to reject the existence of a Creator (Romans 1:20 and Psalm 19:1). A second reason is that evidences of design are clear to all people whatever their age and education. A third reason is that evidence of design provides positive evidence for a Creator rather than negative evidence against a particular man-made theory of origins. Even if the Big Bang theory was proved wrong, this would not stop another atheistic theory from being produced.

(2.6) Admissions by secular science

The problems with the Big Bang theory are so serious that even secular scientific publications sometimes contain very critical reviews of the theory. The following extract, from an article by Oldershaw in *New Scientist*, gives an example of the criticisms made against the Big Bang theory:

'The Big Bang cosmological model has several serious problems …When the original inflation model ran into contradictions, it was replaced by a modification called the "new inflation". When further problems arose, theorists postulated yet another version called "extended inflation". Some have even advocated adding a second inflationary period – "double inflation"…Let us consider some of the problems. First, the Big Bang is treated as an unexplainable event without a cause. Second, the Big Bang could not explain convincingly how matter got organised into lumps (galaxies and clusters of galaxies). And thirdly, it did not predict that for the Universe to be held together in the way it is, more than 90 % of the Universe would have to be in the form of some strange, unknown dark form of matter. Even the strongest piece of evidence for the Big Bang has turned in on it. Matter is not found to be spread out uniformly. Correspondingly, the left-over radiation from the Big Bang should also be inhomogeneous. Unfortunately, the results from the Cosmic Background Explorer (COBE) satellite, recently launched to investigate the microwave background, has revealed that this wash of radiation is relentlessly uniform. So it conflicts with the theoretical Big Bang predictions. Nevertheless the theorists are determined to hang on in there…Theorists also invented the concepts of inflation and cold dark matter to augment the Big Bang paradigm and keep it viable, but they too have come into increasing conflict with observations. In the light of all these problems, it is astounding that the Big Bang hypothesis is the only cosmological model that physicists have taken seriously.'[11]

Notice at the end of this quotation how the author thinks that it is 'astounding' that the Big Bang hypothesis is the only model that physicists have taken seriously. If it is astounding that scientists have such faith in the Big Bang theory, then surely it is also astounding that the Big Bang theory is presented as a fact in schools and universities! The fact that schools and universities are so willing to teach a theory that has so many weaknesses shows that the secular world is committed to an atheistic philosophy. The serious problems with the Big Bang theory also show the folly of the reasoning of many liberal theologians that 'science must be believed'.

Many of the concepts of modern theoretical physics have also been criticised recently. In the New Scientist article quoted above, Oldershaw goes on to make the following criticisms of modern theoretical physics:

'During the past decade or so, two worrying trends have emerged in the two areas of physics that claim to explain the nature of everything – particle physics and cosmology. The first trend is that physicists are increasingly devising mathematically elegant hypotheses, which they say are "compelling" but which nevertheless cannot be verified by experiments or observations. The second trend is that theorists are reluctant to give up their elegant notions, preferring to modify the theory rather than discard it even when observations do not support it…there are many…hypotheses of the "new physics" that suffer from a lack of testable predictions. Some that come to mind are the existence of "hidden dimensions", "shadow matter", "wormholes" in space-time and the "many worlds" interpretation of quantum mechanics. Speculation is a crucial part of scientific progress and it must be encouraged. But without the benefit of predictions, we are in serious danger of ending up with elegant theories that have little or nothing to do with how the real world works...This Platonic attitude worries me – a hypothesis can come to be regarded as being so convincing and elegant that it simply must be right. This then leads researchers to mistrust and neglect observational results that conflict with the hypothesis...Some theorists have openly expressed the view that "physics is almost finished": if these Platonists have their own way physics, as a science, will indeed be finished.'[12]

In this quotation, the writer is clearly arguing that concepts such as 'hidden dimensions', 'shadow matter' and 'worm holes' probably have no place in reality. The writer also makes the very important point that modern theoretical physics has suffered from a gross lack of experimental verification. In engineering, it is a well-known fact that sound knowledge must be based on careful experimentation. Considering the lack of experimentation in modern physics, it is not surprising that many of the concepts do not seem to be based on reality.

The distinguished astronomer Halton Arp has said this about modern theoretical physics:

'In physics, if something is not specially forbidden, it is mandatory.'[13]

Many theoretical physicists seem to work on the principle that they can assume anything in their theories unless there is an extremely strong reason why they cannot. This explains why secular scientists outside of physics have the following saying: 'There is speculation, wild speculation and there is theoretical physics'!

Given that even some secular scientists are very sceptical about the concepts of modern physics and given that modern physics is largely based on atheistic philosophy, we can conclude that Christians should be very cautious about accepting the ideas of modern theoretical physics.

(2.7) Theistic evolution

Some Christians believe that God used a Big Bang to create the Universe over billions of years in exactly the way that the secular Big Bang theory proposes. The idea that God used evolution to create the Universe is sometimes referred to as 'theistic evolution'. A common objection put forward by Christians who support the Big Bang theory is this: 'Why has God made seeming evidence for the Big Bang?'. However, there is a very straightforward answer to this objection: there is no real evidence for the Big Bang theory. As explained previously, even secular scientists can see the weaknesses in the Big Bang theory. The only reason that there is seeming evidence for the Big Bang theory is that secular scientists have deliberately made an atheistic theory of origins that appears to be compatible with the observed features of the Universe. Considering the ingenuity of man (and Satan), it is not surprising that man has invented an elaborate Big Bang cosmology that superficially fits the evidence.

The main problem with the secular Big Bang theory is that it proposes that natural processes and natural timeframes can fully explain how the Universe came into being. A second problem with the Big Bang theory is that it is based on a different order of creation than that revealed in Genesis 1. Whereas the Earth is made after the stars in the Big Bang theory, the Earth is made before the stars in the biblical creation account. A third problem is that the Big Bang theory requires billions of years to generate everything in the Universe whereas the Biblical creation account teaches that only six days were required for creation. In order to overcome the conflicts with Genesis 1, theistic evolutionists argue that Genesis 1 is poetic and, therefore, the details should not be taken literally. However, as described in Chapter 1, we can be certain that Genesis 1 is a literal account of origins. Therefore, old-Earth Big Bang cosmology must be rejected.

2.8 Young-Earth relativistic cosmology

Some Christians have recently proposed the idea that God created the Universe in a natural process which is like the secular Big Bang theory but which is in accord with six-day creation and a young Earth. As described in Chapter 1, this young-Earth relativistic cosmology theory has been described in the book *Starlight and Time*. The relativistic cosmology theory uses natural processes that are similar to those used in the Big Bang such as star formation over billions of years by gravitational attraction of gas clouds. However, by using different starting assumptions and boundary conditions, the order and length of creation is made to be consistent with Genesis 1. The theory also involves God intervening in the natural processes to fine-tune the Universe. However, it is not clear to what extent the natural processes are allowed to run their course and how much God intervenes.

It is commendable that the relativistic cosmology theory is consistent with the order and timing of Genesis 1. In addition, the basic idea that a long history of star events took place in the distant cosmos on Day Four of creation may well be correct. However, as explained in Chapter 1, since supernatural events are outside of natural laws, science *cannot* be used to explain how the Universe came into being. Therefore, if there was a long history of star events on Day Four, then it must have happened supernaturally and not by natural processes. In the same way that science cannot rationalise how water can be supernaturally turned into wine, so science cannot describe how the Universe supernaturally came into being. The problem of trying to explain the miracle of creation in terms of natural processes has been pointed out by DeYoung:

'There have been many attempts to stretch the creation days into vast periods of time in order to accommodate scripture with secular science. However, the problem is not with scripture but with our attempts to rationalise and understand the creation week, something that cannot be done by finite minds![14

One of the reasons why the relativistic cosmology theory was produced was because it was considered that instantaneous creation theories of starlight were inadequate for explaining how we can see distant starlight in a young Universe. However, as explained in Chapter 1, instantaneous creation *can* fully explain how we see distant starlight in a young Universe. Another motivation for the theory was the belief that there is strong evidence for a Big Bang.[15] However, as pointed out many times already, there is no strong evidence to support the Big Bang theory. A perceived problem with starlight and apparent evidence for the Big Bang cannot be a justification for proposing a naturalistic explanation of creation.

Given that scripture *declares* that God spoke the stars into existence and given that God was *able* to speak the stars into existence, it is surely inconceivable that God used a naturalistic method to create the stars. The supernatural manner of creation is confirmed in Hebrews: 'By faith we understand that the worlds were framed by the word of God, so that the things which are seen were not made of the things which are visible.' (Hebrews 11:3). This verse rules out any possibility of scientific understanding being applied to the creation week. We understand origins by 'faith', not by scientific explanations. The worlds were made by the 'word' of God, not by natural processes. The things that are seen (such as stars) were made from 'nothing', not from pre-existing matter that had existed for billions of years.

2.9 The dangers of naturalistic explanations of miracles

There are several dangers with naturalistic explanations of miracles:

❶ Naturalistic explanations inevitably add revelation to scripture

Naturalistic explanations of miracles inevitably involve speculations beyond what is revealed in scripture. The Bible teaches clearly that we should not add revelation to scripture (Revelation 22:18). Naturalistic explanations also tend to be very detailed and this inevitably provides a distraction from scripture. A further problem with naturalistic explanations is that they give the impression that God is constrained by natural laws.

❷ Naturalistic explanations may contain false theories

Naturalistic explanations such as the young-Earth relativistic cosmology theory use several concepts of modern theoretical physics such as a 'white hole', 'inflationary expansion' and 'five dimensions'. Since modern theoretical physics is dominated by atheistic thinking, there is a real possibility that some of these theories are false theories. As explained earlier, such concepts have never been demonstrated in real life and many scientists outside of theoretical physics regard them as wildly speculative. Therefore, there is a real possibility that naturalistic explanations such as the young-Earth relativistic cosmology are based on false theories.

ⓘⓘⓘ Naturalistic explanations tend to be very complicated

The concepts of modern theoretical physics are extremely complicated and abstract. On the one hand, the interpretation that God spoke the stars into existence is very straightforward and can be understood by everyone. On the other hand, the secular Big Bang theory is incomprehensible to ordinary people. (Indeed, there is a case for arguing that Satan has deliberately made modern theoretical physics complicated in order to blind people about the truth of the origins of the Universe.) In the case of the young-Earth relativistic cosmology, it has abandoned straightforward instantaneous creation and has adopted a theory that is just as incomprehensible as the secular Big Bang theory. In fact, the relativistic cosmology theory is so complicated that there is little agreement about the validity of the theory even amongst creationist experts in mathematics.[16] If experts in mathematics cannot agree on the theory, then how can ordinary people begin to understand the theory or make a judgement about whether the theory is right?

ⓘⓥ Naturalistic explanations give respectability to atheistic theories

Another danger with naturalistic explanations is that they inevitably give respectability to atheistic theories of origins. There is a danger that people will see little difference between the young-Earth relativistic cosmology and the secular Big Bang theory.

Some people may argue that instantaneous starlight theories like the created-in-transit theory or speeded-up stars theory also involve 'explanations' of miracles. However, there are two important differences between these theories and naturalistic explanations of origins. Firstly, instantaneous starlight theories do not involve any explanation about the *origin* of the stars. For example, the speeded-up stars theory assumes that the origin of the stars was totally supernatural. Secondly, the theories do not use any naturalistic process to explain how starlight reached the Earth. Therefore, instantaneous starlight theories do not have the problems associated with naturalistic explanations of miracles.

(2.10) God's judgement on modern science

People wonder how scientists can believe the Big Bang theory when there is so little evidence to support it. Part of the answer to this question is that man stubbornly refuses to believe in the existence of a Creator. Another part of the answer is that God 'turns wise men backward, and makes their knowledge foolishness' (Isaiah 44:25). This judgement is appropriate because atheism is itself foolishness. The psalmist reminds us that: 'The fool has said in his heart, "There is no God."' (Psalm 14:1). As time goes by, it is hoped that more teachers and students will come to realise the foolishness of human theories of origins. In contrast, we can be confident that the Word of God is true (John 17:17) and true for all eternity (1 Peter 1:25).

Notes on Chapter 2

1   **Malin, S,** *The Greenwich Guide to Stars, Galaxies and Nebulae*, The National Maritime Museum, London, pp 10-14, 1989.

2   Ref 1, p 16.

3   **Malin, S,** *The Greenwich Guide to The Planets*, The National Maritime Museum, London, pp 7-8, 1987.

4   **Jones, B,** *Astronomy*, Gallery Books, New York, p 7, 1987.

5   **Dick, SJ,** *Life on other worlds*, Cambridge University Press, p 23, 1998.

6   **Jakosky, B,** *The search for life on other planets*, Cambridge University Press, p 15, 1998.

7   Ref 1, p 16.

8   **Atkins, PW,** *The Creation*, Freeman, Oxford, p 9, 1981.

9   Ref 8, pp 3-8.

10   **Burgess, SC,** *Hallmarks of Design*, DayOne Publications, Epsom, Surrey, 2000.

11   **Oldershaw, R**, *What's wrong with the new physics?*, New Scientist, pp 56-59, 22/29 December 1990.

12   Ref 11, p 181.

13   **Arp, H,** *Quasars, Redshifts and Controversies*, Interstellar media, p 3, 1987.

14   **DeYoung, DB,** *Astronomy and the Bible*, Baker, Grand Rapids, Second Edition, pp 39-40, 2000.

15   **Humphreys, R,** *Starlight and Time*, Master Books, Green Forest, p 45, 1994.

16   **Byl, J,** *God and Cosmos*, Banner of Truth, p 193, 2001.

Clockwork motion in the Universe

'He hangs the Earth on nothing' (Job 26:7).

'...He has set a tabernacle for the Sun, which is like a bridegroom coming out of his chamber, and rejoices like a strong man to run its race. Its rising is from one end of heaven, and its circuit to the other end' (Psalm 19:4-6).

For thousands of years, the book of Job has described how God 'hangs the Earth on nothing'. Modern observations have shown the astounding truth of this verse. The Earth is literally suspended in a vacuum and is held in place by the invisible force of gravity as it orbits the Sun. The fact that the book of Job was written several millennia ago, when people did not know about the structure of the Solar System, demonstrates that the Bible has been inspired by the Creator of the Universe.

In Psalm 19, the psalmist describes the clockwork motion involved in the movement of the Earth relative to the Sun. Observations over the last few centuries have confirmed that there is indeed clockwork motion in the Solar System with all of the planets and moons moving with great precision and repeatability. Recent discoveries have also shown that the whole Universe contains amazingly precise and ordered motion in the stars and galaxies. This clockwork motion bears witness to a supremely intelligent Creator. The clockwork motion of the Universe also shows the folly of the idea that the Universe has been produced in a Big Bang.

3.1 Clockwork motion in the Solar System

A schematic diagram of the Solar System is shown in Figure 1. The Earth is

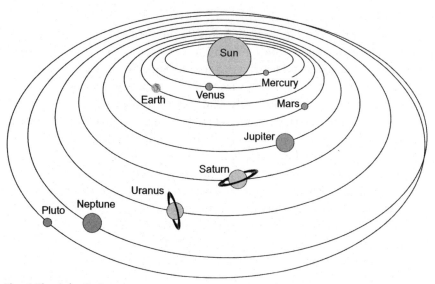

Fig. 1 The Solar System

one of nine planets that go around the Sun. There are also more than 50 moons associated with the nine planets. Jupiter, Saturn and Uranus have more than a dozen moons each, Mars and Neptune have two and Pluto and the Earth have one each. The Solar System also has an asteroid belt between the orbits of Mars and Jupiter. This belt consists of tens of thousands of lumps of material up to about 1000 km in size which are spread throughout a belt which orbits the Sun.

The Solar System is vast in size by any man-made standards. The Earth itself is about 12,700 km in diameter, which is enormous compared with the largest man-made artefact. However, the Earth is tiny in comparison to the size of the Sun and the size of the Solar System. The Sun is about 1.4 million km in diameter and the Solar System is about 15 billion km (15,000,000,000 km) in diameter.[1]

❶ Stable and precise planetary orbits

The planets and moons in the Solar System have remarkably stable and precise motions. If one looks at the Solar System from above the North Pole, then all the planets go around the Sun in an anticlockwise direction as shown in Figure 1. In Figure 1 it should be noted that the orbit of each planet is elliptical not circular. The motion of each planet is just right for keeping the planet in a stable orbit around the Sun. The closer a planet is to the Sun, the shorter time it takes to orbit the Sun. Mercury, which is the closest planet to the Sun, takes only 88 days to make a complete orbit. The Earth, which is the third closest planet to the Sun, takes 365 days to make a complete orbit. Pluto, which is the furthest planet from the Sun, takes about 248.5 years to make a complete orbit.

Secular books on astronomy claim that the circular motion of the Solar System provides evidence that it condensed from a spinning gas cloud. However, designers often put circular motion into machines, so it is wrong to assume that circular motion must be an evidence of evolution. To illustrate this point, consider the scenario of a tourist in London who discovers the Millennium Wheel and wonders how it originated. (The Millennium Wheel is a large circular structure that lifts viewing balconies high up in the sky in central London to enable tourists to view the city of London.) If the tourist concluded from the circular motion that the wheel had condensed out of a gas cloud, this would, of course, be ludicrous. The reason for the circular motion of the Millennium Wheel is that the designers designed it that way because they knew that this gives very stable and precise motion. In a similar way, when people observe the circular motion of the Solar System, it is a great mistake to simply assume that the circular motion is evidence of evolution by natural processes.

There are actually logical reasons why God would want to supernaturally and instantly create the Solar System with orbiting planets. The speed of each planet is such that all the planets are held in near circular orbits by the force of gravity. Without the orbital motion, the Earth and other planets would be pulled into the Sun and be burned up. The fact that there are purposeful design reasons for the motion of the Solar System shows that the circular motion of the Solar System cannot be used as evidence of evolution.

The orbital motions of the planets are so stable and precise that they actually provide great evidence of intelligent design. The main reason for the stability of the orbital motions is that the planets do not get close enough to each other to exert significant gravitational pulls on each other.

There are two reasons why the planets do not get close to each other. The first reason is that the elliptical orbits of most of the planets are not far from being circular. Apart from Mercury and Pluto (the planets that are closest and furthest from the Sun), all the planets have elliptical orbits that are within ±10% of being circular. The fact that the orbits of most of the planets are close to being circular means that, apart from Pluto, none of the planets stray into each other's paths. The second reason why the planets do not interfere with each other is that they are separated by very large distances. The nine planets are spread across a distance of 15 billion km in diameter. Even though some of the planets are very large compared to the Earth, all the planets appear as tiny balls on the scale of the Solar System.

It is very difficult for evolution to explain how a dust cloud, which is at least 15 billion km in diameter, could condense into such a small number of neat planets and moons with extremely precise and stable orbits. According to evolution, the Solar System was formed following millions of random collisions between blobs of matter. However, random collisions tend to cause non-circular blobs of matter and highly elliptical orbits. In addition, there have been no observations of the formation of other solar systems anywhere in the Universe. Therefore, the evolutionist must have faith that the Solar System evolved by chance. Considering the precise motion of the Solar System, an enormous amount of faith is required to believe that the Solar System evolved.

ⓘ Aligned planetary orbits

Figure 1 shows how all nine planets orbit the Sun in approximately the same plane. The fact that all the planets have orbits that lie in the same plane is often quoted as evidence that the Solar System formed from a disc-like gas cloud. But there are at least three important reasons why God would want to make the orbits of all of the planets lie in the same plane. One reason is that a common orbital plane makes the planets move along a clearly defined path in the sky (called the ecliptic) and therefore makes them easy to locate from the Earth. If all the planets were in different planes, then planets would be very difficult to find because they could be anywhere in the night sky. A second reason for making the planets orbit in the same plane is that planet alignment is thus quite common. With all the planets moving in the same plane, it is quite common to get alignment of two or more planets and this alignment of the planets produces quite a striking effect in the night sky. A third reason for making the planets move in the same plane is that this enables the large gas planets (particularly Jupiter) to eject comet-sized bodies from the Solar System by virtue of their gravitational pull.[2] This activity may well be important for the well-being of life on Earth! The fact that there are so many reasons why God would make all the planets have similar orbital planes means that the orbital planes cannot be used as evidence for evolution of the Solar System.

⊕ Irreducible motion

An irreducible motion is a motion that cannot be produced by a gradually changing process. One irreducible motion in the Solar System is found in the spin of the planet Uranus. According to evolution, all the planets should spin such that their axes of spin are approximately parallel to the axis of rotation of the Solar System. The reason for this is that if the Sun and planets had condensed out of an original spinning gas cloud, then all the motions in the Solar System should be in the same direction and with similar axes of rotation. However, despite the logical implication of evolutionary theories, the planet Uranus has an axis of rotation which is almost perpendicular to the axis of the Solar System. The axis of Uranus is actually 98 degrees different to what it should be if the Solar System had evolved. This means that at one position in the Uranus year, the Sun shines directly on the North Pole of Uranus, and at another time of the year the Sun points directly on the South Pole. The planet Venus also has a retrograde rotation, which means that it rotates in the opposite direction to the way the planet goes round the Sun.

Some of the moons in the Solar System also have motions that are inconsistent with evolutionary theories. The four outer moons of Jupiter have retrograde orbits, which means that they orbit Jupiter in the opposite direction to the way the planet goes round the Sun. Triton, one of the moons of the planet Neptune, and Phoebe, one of the moons of Saturn, also have retrograde orbits.

The Solar System contains such stable and intricate motion, that it possesses a higher level of supreme design than man-made machines like the Millennium Wheel. If someone said that they were convinced that the Millennium Wheel had been produced by chance, we would be amazed at their faith and speculation. However, the belief that the Solar System evolved requires an even greater faith. In the same way that the Millennium Wheel bears witness to the skill of human designers, so the Solar System bears witness to the Creator of the Universe.

3.2 Clockwork motion in the Milky Way Galaxy

Our Sun is one star in a galaxy of stars called the Milky Way Galaxy. Astronomers have recently estimated that there are at least 100 billion stars in our Galaxy.[3] On a clear night it is possible to see up to 3,000 stars and all of these stars belong to the Milky Way Galaxy. The reason why we do not see more than 3,000 stars is that most stars in the Galaxy are too far away to be seen with the naked eye. However, with a powerful telescope it is possible to see millions of other stars in our Galaxy.

It is not possible to know exactly what the Milky Way Galaxy looks like because we can only view the Galaxy from the inside. However, by looking at the Galaxy in many different directions from the Earth, astronomers have built up quite a detailed picture of the Galaxy. Looking face-on, the Milky Way Galaxy has the appearance of a spiral shape as shown in Figure 2(a). There are several separate arms, each of which contains billions of stars. Looking from the side, the Milky Way has the shape of a thin disc with a central bulge as shown in Figure 2(b). The Solar System is located about two-thirds of the way out from the centre of the Milky Way Galaxy as shown in Figures 2(a) and 2(b). The location of the Earth in the Galaxy explains why the Earth is completely surrounded by a thin band of sparkling light. This band of light is called the 'Milky Way'.

Even though the Solar System is extremely large, it actually forms a very tiny part of the Milky Way Galaxy. The diameter of the Milky Way Galaxy is about one billion billion km (1,000,000,000,000,000,000 km), which is about 100 million times bigger than the diameter of the Solar System. Even the closest stars to the Earth are a vast distance away. The nearest star to the Solar System is called Proxima Centauri and it is about 40 thousand billion km away.

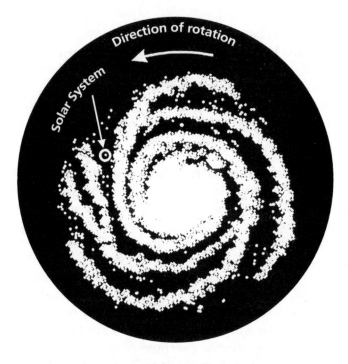

Fig. 2a View of the Milky Way Galaxy from the front

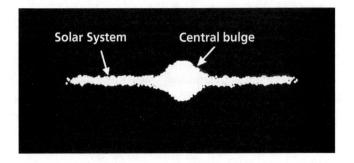

Fig. 2b View of the Milky Way Galaxy from the side

Fig. 2 The Milky Way Galaxy

❶ Stable and precise orbits

Like the Solar System, the Milky Way Galaxy has a remarkably stable and precise motion. The Galaxy has a dense nucleus of stars at its centre and the entire Galaxy slowly rotates around this nucleus in much the same way that the planets rotate around the Sun. The only difference is that the Galaxy rotates extremely slowly. In Figure 2(a), the Galaxy is shown rotating in the anticlockwise direction as shown. The velocity of each star depends on how far it is from the centre, with the outer stars having the slowest rotational speed. The Solar System travels around the centre of the Milky Way Galaxy with a linear velocity of about 220 km per second. Even though the outer stars in the Galaxy are moving very fast, the vast size of the Galaxy means that it would take over 200 million years for the Galaxy to rotate just once!

According to the Big Bang theory, the Milky Way Galaxy has evolved by chance from a slowly spinning gas cloud over billions of years. The fact that the Galaxy is now known to be slowly spinning is used as evidence for evolution. But this evidence again ignores the fact that intelligent designers often use rotation in machines. There are very logical reasons why God would make the Milky Way Galaxy rotate around a central hub. The stars in the Galaxy orbit the hub in such a way that gravity keeps the stars in a stable orbit. This means that there is no danger that our Sun will be pulled to the central hub where it would certainly collide with other stars. In addition, it means that our Sun will not be thrown out of the Galaxy. Also, the fact that the billions of stars travel in the same direction helps to prevent collisions between stars. The fact that there are logical design reasons for the motion of the Milky Way Galaxy shows that there is no justification for using the rotation of the Galaxy as evidence for evolution. In fact, the circular motion of the Galaxy is so stable that it provides great evidence for intelligent design.

❷ Irreducible motion

According to evolution, the Milky Way Galaxy has condensed from a gas cloud over 15 billion years and therefore the Galaxy should have rotated numerous times with the inner part rotating many times more than the outer part. Evolutionists admit that the inner part of the galaxy should have rotated over one hundred times and the outer part about 50 times.[4]

This means that the Galaxy should not have spiral arms but should contain a large number of concentric circles. However, from Figure 2(a) it can be seen that the Galaxy does have spiral arms. In addition, the arms are only slightly bent and this means that the inner stars have only rotated more than the outer stars by a fraction of one turn. From the shape of the Milky Way Galaxy it can be concluded that the Galaxy has not evolved over billions of years. To solve the problem of having the 'wrong evidence', scientists have proposed a 'density wave' theory that involves stars slowing down and queuing in a similar way to which cars slow down and queue in slow-moving traffic. However, this theory has no experimental verification and it is doubtful whether there can be an analogy with traffic since stars do not have 'drivers' to slow them down! The 'density wave' theory is an example of where modern scientists propose new theories as soon as the evidence does not support the Big Bang theory.

(3.3) Clockwork motion of galaxies in the Universe

Figure 3 summarises the structure of the Universe, showing the place of the Solar System in the Milky Way Galaxy and the place of the Milky Way Galaxy in the Universe. Each tiny white patch in the picture of the Universe in Figure 3 represents an entire galaxy of stars. Galaxies are like islands in space, separated from other galaxies by vast distances. Most galaxies are part of clusters of galaxies. For example, the Milky Way Galaxy is part of a local cluster of about 30 galaxies. Astronomers estimate that there are over 50 billion galaxies in the Universe. In addition, they estimate that each galaxy contains at least a billion stars. As well as containing a fantastic number of stars, the Universe is also absolutely vast in size. Astronomers estimate that the observable Universe is three hundred thousand billion billion km (300,000,000,000,000,000,000,000 km) in diameter, which is about three hundred thousand times larger than the Milky Way Galaxy!

To get an idea of the vast size of the Universe it is helpful to consider the following illustrations of scale. Firstly, if the Solar System was reduced in size by a factor of one billion then the Earth would be just under 1.3 cm in diameter, the Sun would be about 1.4 m in diameter,

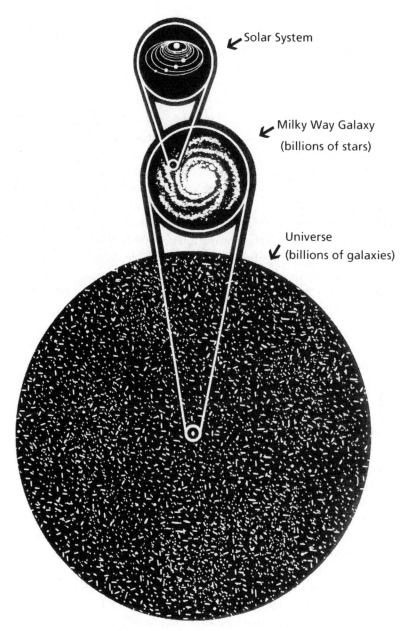

Solar System

Milky Way Galaxy
(billions of stars)

Universe
(billions of galaxies)

Fig. 3 The place of the Solar System and Milky Way Galaxy in the Universe

the Earth's orbit would be about 300 m in diameter and the Solar System would be about 15 km in diameter. Secondly, if the Milky Way Galaxy was reduced in size by a factor of one million billion then the Solar System would be about 1.5 cm in diameter, the nearest star (Proxima Centauri) would be about 40 m away and the Milky Way Galaxy would be about 1,000 km in diameter. Thirdly, if the Universe was reduced in size by a factor of one hundred thousand billion billion then the Milky Way Galaxy would be about 1 cm in diameter, the Andromeda Galaxy would be about 25 cm away and the Universe would be about 3 km in diameter.

In the first half of the twentieth century, astronomers discovered evidence that all the galaxies in the Universe are moving away from each other. The astronomer Edwin Hubble also produced a theory (now known as Hubble's law) that the further away a galaxy is from the Earth, the faster it appears to be receding from our own Milky Way Galaxy. Many astronomy books claim that the expansion of the Universe is evidence of the aftermath of a Big Bang. One astronomy book presents the evidence like this:

'If the galaxies are getting further apart at present, then they must have previously been closer together. As we go back in time they get closer and closer together until we reach a time when everything in the Universe was jam-packed together into a super dense blob.'[5]

In this quotation, the author assumes that the Universe is billions of years old and that this means that the galaxies 'must have' been closer together. However, if the assumption of old age is incorrect, then this would mean that the galaxies were not close together in the past. This is an example of how the Big Bang theory is based on philosophical assumptions that cannot be proven.

There is actually a logical reason why God would want to make the Universe as an expanding Universe in that the expansion of galaxies gives the Universe stability. Measurements of the expansion indicate that it is at just the right level to make the Universe perfectly stable. On the one hand, if there were no expansion, the galaxies would pull together and collapse. On the other hand, if the expansion were too fast, then the Universe would fly apart. The expansion appears to be such that it will slow down gradually but never actually go into reverse. The fact that expansion can have a purpose shows that there is no reason to assume that there has been a Big Bang. In fact, the expansion appears to be so finely tuned that it can actually be seen as evidence of design.

(3.4) The position of the Earth in the Universe

The fact that the Earth is centre-stage of the Universe, in a spiritual sense, raises the question of whether the Earth is at the exact 'geographical centre' of the Universe. The first thing to say in answer to this question is that the Bible does not teach that the Earth is at the exact geographical centre of the Universe. The Earth can be at the centre of God's purposes in the Universe no matter where the Earth is located. In the last few centuries, observations have shown that the Earth cannot be at the exact geographical centre of the Universe because the Earth is not stationary. It goes round the Sun and the whole Solar System is going round the Milky Way Galaxy.

Even though the Earth is not at the exact geographical centre of the Universe, there is good reason to believe that the Earth is not that far from being so. Since the Universe has a function of serving the Earth, it is reasonable to assume that the Milky Way Galaxy is 'approximately' at the centre of the Universe as shown in Figure 3.

Notes on Chapter 3

1   15 billion km is approximately double the maximum distance between Pluto and the Sun.

2   **Brunier, S,** *Majestic Universe,* Cambridge University Press, p 76, 1999.

3   Ref 2, p 26.

4   **Malin, S,** *The Greenwich Guide to Stars, Galaxies and Nebulae,* The National Maritime Museum, London, p 62, 1989.

5   Ref 4, P 10.

How the Earth is designed for life

'For thus says the Lord, who created the heavens, who is God, who formed the Earth and made it, who has established it, who did not create it in vain, who formed it to be inhabited: I am the Lord, and there is no other' (Isaiah 45:18).

The book of Isaiah teaches that the Earth has been specially prepared to be inhabited. Discoveries in the modern age have shown the spectacular truth of this verse. The Earth has every single one of the many features required for life. In contrast, every other known planet is far too hostile to have any possibility of supporting life.

(4.1) Life-supporting features of the Earth

There are many features associated with the Earth which make it ideally suited for life. Fifteen of the most important features are summarised below:

❶ Right rate of spin

The Earth has the right rate of spin for producing day and night. It is easy to take the 24-hour day for granted but it is an important property that is ideally suited to life on Earth. If the days were much longer, they would get too hot and the nights would get too cold. If the days were much shorter, then there would be violent weather conditions due to the increased speed of the Earth. Another ideal aspect of the 24-hour day is that it is just right for sleep and rest for creatures.

⑪ Right length of year

The length of a year is just right because it produces winters that are just short enough for creatures to survive on stocks of food and energy. The yearly cycle of seasons is also long enough to enable plants to produce crops of food in the summer.

⑫ Right tilt on the axis of rotation

The axis of rotation of the Earth has an ideal angle of tilt to produce the seasons of spring, summer, autumn and winter.[1] The intricate motion and orientation of the Earth is shown in Figure 4(a). The Earth goes round the Sun at the rate of approximately once per 365 days (one Earth year). The Earth also spins on its axis in the anticlockwise direction once per day and this causes the night and day cycle with the Sun rising in the east and setting in the west. The axis of rotation of the Earth is tilted at an angle of 23.5 degrees with respect to the axis of the orbit around the Sun. This means that from April to September, the Northern Hemisphere receives the Sun's rays more directly, as shown in Figure 4(b), so that the northern summer occurs. From October to March, the Southern Hemisphere receives the Sun's rays more directly so that the southern summer occurs, as shown in Figure 4(b). The midsummer position for the Northern Hemisphere occurs on 21 June and is called the summer solstice. The midwinter position for the Northern Hemisphere occurs on 21 December and is called the winter solstice. In between these points are the spring and autumn equinox on 21 March and 21 September respectively. The cycle of seasons that is produced by the Earth's tilt is very important for life on Earth. The cycle of winter and summer is what triggers the timing of processes such as blossoming in plants and courtship in creatures. Without the Earth's tilt, there would be no seasons and no timing triggers for living organisms. The level of tilt is also just right for life. On the one hand, if the tilt were much more than 23.5 degrees, then there would be the problem of great ice caps melting in summertime. On the other hand, if the tilt were much less than 23.5 degrees, then there would not be enough variation in temperature and light to make different seasons.

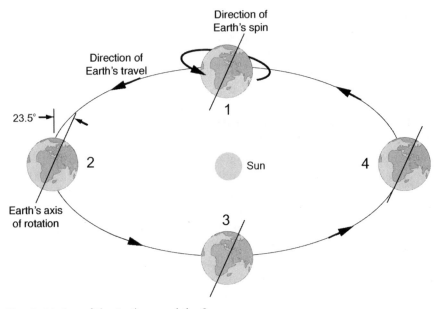

Fig. 4a Motion of the Earth around the Sun

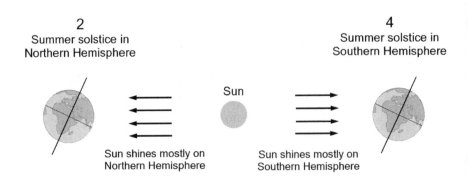

Fig. 4b Position of the Earth in summertime

Fig. 4 The motion of the Earth

ⓘⓥ Right distance from Sun

The average distance between the Earth and the Sun is about 150 million km, which produces the right average temperature on the Earth. Scientists have calculated that if the Earth were just 10% closer to the Sun, then it would be like a furnace.[2] On the other hand, if it were 20% further away from the Sun, then it would be like an icy desert. The Earth has an average temperature of about 15 degrees Celsius which is ideal for life.[3] The fact that scientists are worried about the effect of global warming of just one or two degrees shows how ideal the present average temperature is. The fact that people live on almost every part of the planet also shows that the distance between the Earth and the Sun is just right.

ⓥ Right orbit

Not only is the Earth at the right average distance from the Sun, but it also has a nearly circular orbit. The distance between the Earth and the Sun varies between about 147 and 152 million km which represents a small variation. The variation in distance from the Sun is so small that it has very little effect on the amount of heat that the Earth receives from the Sun. This means that the only significant cause of heating and cooling comes from the effect of the tilt of the Earth's axis.

ⓥⓘ Right surface smoothness

The Earth has a remarkably smooth surface. Even the highest mountains and deepest oceans represent very small variations compared to the diameter of the Earth. The largest variation in surface smoothness at the highest mountain or deepest sea is about 0.1% of the diameter. In most places, the variation in surface smoothness is less than 0.01%. If a small-scale model of the Earth were to be made measuring 1 metre in diameter, the highest mountain would be less than 1 mm high. The smoothness of the Earth is very important for giving the Earth suitable oceans and weather patterns. For example, if the mountains were ten times higher, then there would be extreme local weather conditions. It is very difficult for evolution to explain how the Earth is so smooth. Recall how evolutionists believe that the planets were formed by random collisions of matter. No one has ever seen random collisions of millions of small blobs produce a smooth ball!

⑦ Right diameter

The size of the Earth is just right for life to exist because it produces the right level of gravity. On the one hand, if the Earth were much smaller, then this would adversely affect biological processes that rely on significant amounts of gravity such as bone growth. On the other hand, if the Earth were too big, then bones would be under too much stress due to the large forces produced by the high gravitational pull. The level of gravity is also ideal for walking and running. The problems caused by the wrong level of gravity were demonstrated when astronauts were on the Moon. The astronauts found that they did not have much grip on the ground because of the low level of gravity and this made it very difficult to move.

⑧ Right temperature of Earth's surface

The temperature of the Earth's surface is critical. If it were too hot, then excessive water vapour and carbon dioxide would collect in atmospheric clouds and the greenhouse effect would run away with itself causing the ice-caps to melt. If it were too cold, then more snow and ice would form, reflecting solar energy and promoting even cooler temperatures.

⑨ Right amount of water

The Earth has the right amount of water to support abundant life. Compared with other parts of the Solar System, the Earth has an extremely large amount of water in the liquid state. The oceans make up about 70% of the surface of the Earth and there is also a vast network of river channels on the land. The whole water cycle is such that there is a convenient and regular supply of fresh water in nearly every part of the Earth.

⑩ Right materials

The Earth's surface contains a wide range of materials and energy resources. Apart from useful organic materials such as wood and leather, there are abundant metals and ceramics in the ground. Metals provide a very useful set of materials for all kinds of uses. There is a whole range of metals including copper, tin, lead, zinc, aluminium, iron, magnesium, titanium, silver and gold. The range of metals is such that there are materials to satisfy virtually every need of mankind. It is also significant that the most useful materials are also the most abundant in the Earth. For example, iron and aluminium are much more abundant than tungsten and titanium and are also of much more use. The variety, usefulness and appropriate abundance of materials in the Earth give great evidence of design.

ⓧⓘ Right atmosphere

The air in the Earth's atmosphere is made up of the following gases: 78% nitrogen, 21% oxygen, approximately 1% argon and very tiny amounts of carbon dioxide, methane, helium, hydrogen, krypton, neon, ozone and xenon. This composition is just right to support life on Earth. In addition, the Earth's ecosystem requires this composition to remain within quite narrow limits in order to sustain life. For example, too much oxygen would give oxygen poisoning to creatures whilst too little would make breathing difficult. Also, too much oxygen would cause significant problems with spontaneous combustion. On the other hand, too much carbon dioxide would cause the Earth to overheat whilst too little would prevent plants carrying out photosynthesis.

ⓧⓘⓘ Right ozone layer

High up in the Earth's atmosphere there is an ideal layer of ozone. Recent problems of damage to the ozone layer through man-made pollution have highlighted the importance of the ozone layer.

ⓧⓘⓘⓘ Right magnetic field

The Earth has a magnetic field around it and this plays an important part in deflecting the solar radiation from the Sun. In addition, the magnetic field is useful for navigation for both man and creatures.

ⓧⓘⓥ Right brightness of sky

When the Sun is high in the sky on a cloudless day, the sky is gloriously bright. Even on a cloudy day there is enough brightness to penetrate through the clouds and make a reasonable amount of light. The reason why we have a sky that looks bright in the daytime is because of the Earth's atmosphere. In particular, it is the interaction between sunlight and air molecules in the Earth's atmosphere that causes the sky to light up. When light from the Sun hits the Earth's atmosphere, the light is scattered by air molecules in all directions and bounces off other air molecules so that the entire sky is lit up. If light were not scattered, then the sky would appear black in the daytime everywhere except in the direction of the Sun. The effect of not having an atmosphere can be seen with the Moon. When standing on the Moon in daylight, astronauts observed that the sky was black everywhere except when looking directly at the Sun. In addition, the Sun was extremely bright and hot. In contrast, the sunlight that hits the Earth is spread across the whole of the Earth's sky because of the scattering effect of the atmosphere.

ⓧⓥ Right colour of sky

Not only does scattering light up the sky, but it also lights up the sky with the right colour! The blue sky is just right for the Earth because it gives a contrasting colour to the green land. The Earth's sky is made blue because air molecules in the Earth's atmosphere preferentially scatter shorter wavelengths of light from the white light spectrum of sunlight. Since blue has the shortest wavelength in the colour spectrum, blue is preferentially scattered.

(4.2) Supreme design in the Moon

The Moon plays an important role in the Earth's ecosystem because it causes the tidal system in the oceans. The Moon is so large that it exerts enough pull on the oceans to produce tides of several metres on the shorelines around the world. One of the most important features of the Moon is that it is just the right size for producing suitable levels of tides on the Earth. On the one hand, if the Moon were much bigger, then the tides would be so big that dangerous tidal waves would be produced daily in many places around the world. On the other hand, if the Moon were much smaller, then the tides would hardly be noticeable. Tides are very useful for several reasons. Tides prevent the oceans from becoming too stagnant by causing the waters to be mixed. Tides enable rich life to exist on shorelines because they continually expose food in shallow pools on beaches. Tides help to keep coastlines clean by the washing action of the waves and help to produce useful materials like pebbles and sand. Another function of tides, which should not be omitted, is that they produce enjoyable recreation for people.

An unusual feature of the Moon is that it is very large compared to the size of its parent planet, the Earth. The diameter of the Moon is about 3,500 km which is just over a quarter that of the Earth. This proportion is greater than for any of the other planets. This statistic indicates that the Moon really has been made for the purpose of serving the Earth. The origin of the Moon is a great problem for the evolutionist. Some evolutionary explanations for the Earth's Moon have been bizarre in the extreme. One theory suggests that the Moon was originally a large body that was floating through space and just happened to narrowly miss the Earth in such a way that it got captured by the Earth's orbit. This theory lacks scientific credibility because scientists now know that satellites require precise propulsion systems to enable them to achieve an orbital path. Since the Moon does not have a propulsion system, it could not have produced its own orbit! Another theory of the Moon's origin is that it was originally a large rock that emanated from the Pacific Ocean and is still receding gradually from the Earth today. However, the Moon is so big and makes such a precise orbit around the Earth that it must have been a fully functioning orbiting body from the moment of its creation. For a more detailed study of the Moon the reader is referred elsewhere.[4]

4.3 The uniqueness of the Earth

The other planets in the Solar System help us to appreciate how amazingly well the Earth is designed. Table 1 summarises the main characteristics of the surfaces of the other eight planets in the Solar System. Only the Earth has the right temperature and type of surface for life. Only the Earth has a suitable atmosphere and only the Earth has a clear blue sky! All of the other planets in the Solar System have been visited by spacecraft and they have been found to be very inhospitable.

TABLE 1   CONDITIONS OF PLANETS IN THE SOLAR SYSTEM

PLANET	TEMPERATURE	SURFACE	SKY COLOUR
Mercury	350°C	Rocky	Black
Venus	480°C	Rocky	Dark clouds
The Earth	**15°C average**	**Fertile land/ water**	**Clear blue/ white clouds**
Mars	−23°C average	Rocky	Orange
Jupiter	−150°C	Gas	Orange cloud
Saturn	−180°C	Gas	Yellow cloud
Uranus	−210°C	Gas	Blue-green cloud
Neptune	−220°C	Gas	Blue cloud
Pluto	−230°C	Not known	Not known

Sir Isaac Newton said the following about the Solar System:

'Atheism is so senseless. When I look at the Solar System, I see the Earth at the right distance from the Sun to receive the proper amounts of heat and light. This did not happen by chance.'5

Sir Isaac Newton probably made a greater contribution to physics than any other scientist, so his statement must be taken seriously. If Newton had lived in the present age when we know many more of the wonderful details of the natural world, then his convictions would certainly have been even greater.

Notes on Chapter 4

1   The Earth's climate is now probably different to what it was like before the great Flood at the time of Noah. The reason for this is that the Bible indicates that there was a vapour canopy before the Flood. There is also evidence that the North and South Poles used to have a sub-tropical climate because of the existence of fossils and coal at these places. It is also possible that the seasons of winter, spring, summer and autumn as we know them may only have existed following the Flood (Genesis 8:22). Even though the Earth's climate changed following the Flood, it is still true to say that the positioning of the Earth's axis is ideal for producing seasons and that it represents evidence of supremely intelligent design.

2   **Brunier, S,** *Majestic Universe*, Cambridge University Press, p 76, 1999.

3   Before the Flood it is likely that there were fewer extremes of temperature because of the insulating effect of the water canopy. In particular, it is very likely that there were no freezing temperatures. Given the current design of the Earth's climate, 15 degrees Celsius can still be regarded as an ideal 'average' temperature.

4   **Whitcomb, JC, and DeYoung, DB,** *The Moon: its Creation, Form and Significance*, BMH books, p 141, 1978.

5   **Lamont, A,** *21 Great Scientists who Believed*, Creation Science Foundation, p 47, 1995.

How the stars are designed for the Earth

'He made the stars also. God set them in the firmament of the heavens to give light on the Earth.' (Genesis 1:16-17)

Genesis 1:17 teaches that God 'set' the stars in their place in order to give light on the Earth. Modern discoveries have demonstrated the astounding truth of this verse because it has been found that the stars are indeed the right distance from the Earth for shining just the right amount of light on the Earth. The billions of stars in the Milky Way Galaxy are close enough to make beautiful patterns in the sky, but not so close that they overwhelm the night sky with light. The billions of galaxies in the Universe are close enough to the Earth to be seen in outline but not so close that they make the night sky too bright. Not only do the stars make a beautiful sight, but they are also well designed to help man in practical ways such as indicating seasons. The Bible tells us that the stars are 'for signs and seasons, and for days and years' (Genesis 1:14).

Despite such overwhelming evidences of design, secular astronomers totally reject the idea that the stars are designed to shine light on the Earth. Astronomers do not deny that the Earth has an ideal position in the Universe, but they insist that it must have 'happened by chance'. One of the sad consequences of this atheistic philosophy is that the general public is not told about the many ways in which the Earth has an ideal position in the Universe. This chapter presents some of the fascinating evidences of design that modern day astronomers refuse to acknowledge. These evidences of design are profoundly important because they relate directly to the purpose of the stars as revealed in Genesis 1.

5.1 Perfect daylight

It is very easy to take daylight for granted. However, the Sun is very well designed for the Earth. One of the ideal features of the Sun is that it produces just enough brightness to light up the whole sky, but not so much brightness that it makes the daytime too bright. Another ideal feature of the Sun is that it does not oscillate between a large and small size as some other stars do. When a star produces more energy internally than it can dissipate externally, then the star expands. Also, when a star produces less energy internally than it radiates away, then the star contracts. Many stars do not stabilise at an equilibrium size but oscillate between large and small. The North Star, Polaris, is an example of a star which oscillates significantly in size. If our Sun was a star which oscillated like Polaris, then the Sun would alternate between being far too hot and bright to being far too cold and dim. The fact that our Sun is stable in size is a feature of the Sun that is necessary for life on Earth. Another feature of the Sun that is ideal is that it is yellow-white which is the best colour for producing a bright sky.

(5.2) Ideal brightness of stars

It is also easy to take the lights in the night sky for granted, but the stars are wonderfully designed for the Earth. Stars are neither too bright nor too dim. There are at least three reasons why it is important that the stars are not too bright. Firstly, if the stars were too bright, then there would not be a proper contrast between the night and the day. Secondly, if the nearby stars were too bright, then it would be much more difficult or even impossible to see distant stars and galaxies. Thirdly, if the stars were too bright, then it would be possible to see the stars during the daytime. Since God has made the Sun to rule the day, it is important that we do not see stars during the daytime. It is interesting to note that the Moon is sometimes visible during the daytime. However, the Moon is never very prominent in the daytime because the Moon cannot be more than a half Moon due to the relative positions of the Sun, Earth and Moon during the day. In addition, as the Moon gets closer to the Sun, as viewed from the Earth, the portion of the Moon which reflects the Sun's rays, becomes less and less.

There are also reasons why the stars should not be too dim. One reason is that the stars must be seen clearly if they are to be good for 'signs, seasons, days and years'. A second reason is that the brightness of the stars is an important factor in their clarity and beauty. The following sections describe how the Moon, planets and stars are indeed not too bright and not too dim, but that they have a perfect level of brightness for the Earth.

5.3 Ideal brightness of Moon and planets in the Solar System

The other planets in the Solar System can be seen from the Earth because they reflect light from the Sun. The planets Mars, Jupiter and Saturn are bright enough to be seen with the naked eye at night-time. The planets Mercury and Venus can also be seen with the naked eye although they can only be seen in the evening near sunset and in the morning near sunrise. The reason for this is that at night-time it is only possible to look in a direction which is away from the Sun and therefore it is only possible to see planets that are further from the Sun than the Earth. The planets Uranus, Neptune and Pluto are so far away from the Earth that they usually require a telescope for observation. There are two main features that enable planets to be distinguished from stars. One feature is that planets change in their position relative to the stars from month to month because of the way planets orbit the Sun. Another feature that is special to planets is that their brightness varies significantly because of the way their distance from the Earth changes. Despite the differences with stars, planets have a range of brightness that is remarkably similar to the range of brightness found in the stars.

There are many features that are finely tuned in the Solar System in order to produce the right amount of light. Some of the main features are summarised as follows:

❶ Right apparent brightness of the Moon

The apparent brightness of the Moon is just right because it is dim enough to keep the night-time reasonably dark, but it is bright enough to be clearly superior to the stars and planets. The apparent brightness of the Moon and stars compared to the Sun is shown in Figure 5. The Moon has a brightness which is about three millionths that of the Sun. In contrast, the brightest star (Sirius) has a brightness of less than one ten billionth that of the Sun. One of the reasons why the Moon must be clearly visible is that the Moon is used as a calendar and, therefore, it must be very easy to locate in the sky. The Bible teaches that the Moon was deliberately made to 'rule the night' so it was purposely made to have a brightness that is on a different level to that of the stars.

⓲ Right reflectivity of the Moon

The apparent brightness of the Moon is not just dependent on its size but also on how much the surface reflects light from the Sun. The Moon has a reflectivity of 7%, which means that only 7% of the sunlight that hits the Moon is reflected away from the surface. This amount of reflectivity is just right for giving the Moon the right level of apparent brightness. Since the Moon must be a particular size in order to produce the right level of tides, the reflectivity of the Moon must be tuned to the right level for the Moon to produce the correct brightness. The technical term for the degree of reflectivity of a surface is albedo. The reflectivity of the Moon is quite unusual because it is so low. Many of the planets and moons in the Solar System have levels of reflectivity of between 30 - 80%. For example, the Earth has a reflectivity of about 39% and Venus has a reflectivity of about 76%. If the Moon had a reflectivity of 76%, then it would be over ten times brighter and the night would no longer be dark when a full Moon was shining. The actual level of reflectivity of the Moon is perfectly tuned for the needs of mankind and other life on Earth.

⓲ Right apparent brightness of the planets

The planets have an ideal range of apparent brightness because it is very similar to the range of apparent brightness of the stars. Only the planets Venus, Jupiter and Mars can appear brighter than the stars during the night-time and even in these cases there is not a significant difference in brightness. The fact that planets have a similar brightness to the stars is ideal because it means that the planets do not dominate the stars and the planets do not compete with the Moon. To avoid being too bright in the night sky, the planets must not come too close to the Earth, especially if they are very big. This requirement is exactly met in the Solar System.

To illustrate the ideal positioning of the planets, it is worth considering what would happen if the planet Jupiter were located as close to the Earth as the planet Mars. Since Mars is about ten times closer than Jupiter (at the closest encounter), and since apparent brightness varies with the inverse square of distance, the planet Jupiter would be about one hundred times brighter if it were located as close as Mars. This level of brightness is plotted in Figure 5 to show how it would then compare with the Moon and the stars. Figure 5 shows that if Jupiter were located as close as Mars, it would be very much brighter than the stars and not much different to the Moon. Such a scenario would mean that the Moon would not 'rule the night' and the lighting would not be ideal. Another problem with having such a very bright planet is that it would be visible in the daytime sky for long periods. Unlike the Moon, such a bright planet would appear as a complete disc in the day and could have a position not far away from the Sun. Such a scenario would mean that the Sun would not 'rule the day'.

5.4 Ideal brightness of stars in the Milky Way Galaxy

Even though the Milky Way contains over 100 billion stars, these stars are perfectly positioned and sized to give the Earth the right amount of starlight at night. There are at least nine features in the Milky Way that are finely tuned to make the stars shine light on the Earth in just the right way:

❶ Milky Way Galaxy is the right shape

The thin disc-shape of the Milky Way Galaxy (Figure 2(b)) is ideal because it means that the Earth's night sky is not dominated by dense patches of stars. When looking into the plane of the Milky Way Galaxy, there are millions of stars in view and these combine to form the sparkling band of light that completely circles the Earth. In contrast, when looking in a direction out of the plane of the Milky Way Galaxy, the view may contain only thousands of stars and the sky is relatively dark. The thin disc-shape of the Galaxy has three specific advantages. Firstly, since most of the sky is free of the dense part of the Milky Way Galaxy, it is possible to see many other galaxies.

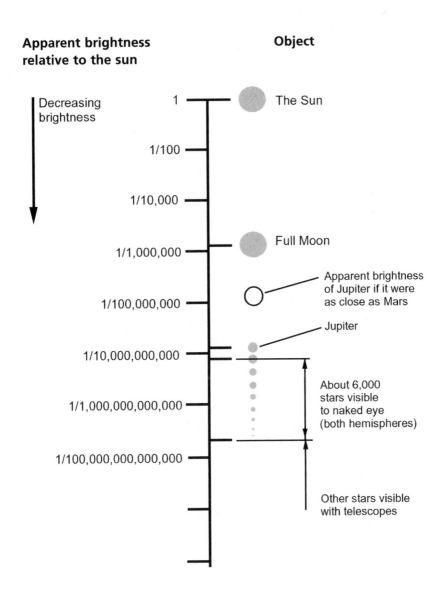

Fig. 5 The apparent brightness of the planets and stars as viewed from the Earth

Secondly, many star patterns and gas clouds often appear at their best when contrasted with the blackness of deep space. Thirdly, the thin band of light of the Milky Way is in itself a sight of outstanding beauty.

ⓚ Solar System away from the centre of Galaxy

The Solar System is positioned about two-thirds of the way out from the centre of the Galaxy, which is far enough away from the galactic bulge to keep the night sky dark. At the centre of the Galaxy there are billions of stars in a relatively small area called the galactic bulge. If the Sun and Earth were near the centre of the Galaxy, there would be many stars in close proximity and the night sky would be so bright it would not be much different from the day. The effect of being located in the galactic bulge has been described by Brunier:

'In our immediate vicinity there may be just about two stars in a cube 10 light-years on a side. In the galactic nucleus, the same volume probably contains more than 10,000 stars! Seen from a planet orbiting one of the stars in this region, the sky must be ablaze: a blinding cloud of thousands of stars as bright as Venus, Jupiter or Sirius in our own sky. Nothing of the outside Universe would be visible, apart from these stars.'[1]

Brunier makes the correct conclusion that if the Earth were located in the galactic bulge, the night sky would be 'ablaze' with light. This quotation shows how Big Bang cosmologists are fully aware that the Earth has an ideal location. However, this remarkable fact is not considered to be significant because secular astronomers assume that the Earth's position was determined by chance.

ⓛ Earth not too near the edge of Galaxy

Near the edge of the Galaxy the stars are spread far apart. If the Sun and Earth were located right on the edge of the Galaxy, then the night sky would be extremely dark in one direction with only a few stars visible. The actual position of the Earth is perfect for receiving the right amount of light at all times of the year.

⓲ Stars spaced at right distance

Another remarkable feature of the Milky Way Galaxy is that the stars are spaced apart at the right distance for producing the correct amount of light for the Earth. On the one hand, if the stars in the Galaxy were much closer together, then the night sky would be too bright. On the other hand, if the stars were much further apart, then the night sky would be too dark. The actual spacing not only gives just the right level of brightness, but also reveals a number of stars that is just right for comprehending when viewed with the naked eye. From each hemisphere it is possible to see about 3,000 stars, which is just the right number for making clear patterns. The perfect design of star spacing can be illustrated by considering what would happen if the Milky Way Galaxy were a thousand times smaller or larger. On the one hand, if the Galaxy were a thousand times smaller, the billions of stars would occupy a space of only one million billion km in diameter. In this case, it would be possible to see millions of stars with the naked eye and the night-time sky would be nearly as bright as the day. On the other hand, if the Galaxy were a thousand times larger, the 100 billion stars would occupy a space of one thousand billion billion km across. In this case, it would not be possible to see any stars with the naked eye and the night sky would be pitch black except when the Moon was shining. The actual density of stars in the Galaxy is perfect for the night sky.

ⓥ Stars not uniformly spaced

If stars were uniformly spaced with the same distance between each one, there would be no distinctive star patterns in the sky and the sky would look monotonous in every direction. However, the actual spacing is very non-uniform and this produces varied and beautiful patterns in the sky such as the Bear, Orion and the Pleiades.

ⓥⓘ The stars are the right colour

The colour of stars can be blue, white, yellow or red. However, the colour of the stars is dominated by white and yellow when viewed with the naked eye from the Earth. This colour scheme is perfect because white and yellow contrast well with the black background of the night sky and this makes the stars easy to see with the naked eye. There are enough red and blue stars to give variety when looking through telescopes, but not so many that we cannot see a large number of white and yellow stars.

ⓥⓘⓘ No large dust clouds too near the Earth

The Milky Way Galaxy contains some large dense patches of dust that stretch for millions of kilometres in space. These dust clouds prevent stars behind the cloud from being seen from the Earth. If there were a large dust cloud near to the Earth, it could completely obscure very large parts of the night sky and make it virtually pitch black. However, none of the large dust clouds in the Milky Way Galaxy are too close to the Earth and there are hence no large areas in the sky which appear black.

ⓥⓘⓘⓘ No stars are too close to the Earth

Astronomers have found that many stars have other stars as close neighbours. However, there are no stars that are very close to our Solar System. The closest star to the Earth apart from our Sun, Proxima Centauri, is about 40 thousand billion km away. If there were stars that were much closer than this, then the night sky could be dominated by extremely bright lights. The ideal positioning and size of the stars local to the Earth shows remarkable evidence of design.

ⓘⓧ No super-giant stars are near to the Earth

As well as having the right distance from the nearest stars, the Solar System is also positioned so that it has the right distance from very bright stars such as super-giant stars. Super-giant stars are a special kind of star that can be over one thousand times larger than the Sun. With such a large size, these stars are extremely bright and could dominate the night sky if any were close to the Earth. Astronomers have found that the closest super-giant stars are very much further from the Earth than the closest ordinary stars. This means that the closest super-giant stars appear not much brighter in the sky than ordinary stars. For example, in the constellation of Orion there is a super-giant star called Rigel, which lies at a distance of about 800 light-years. This distance is about two hundred times further away than the closest star, Proxima Centauri. The distance to

Rigel is just far enough away to prevent Rigel being too bright in the sky.

To illustrate the ideal positioning of Rigel it is useful to consider what would happen if Rigel were as close to the Solar System as Proxima Centauri. Since apparent brightness is related to the area of a star, apparent brightness changes with the inverse square of the distance. This means that Rigel would appear 40 thousand times brighter if it were as close to the Solar System as Proxima Centauri. Since Rigel is already a very bright star in the sky, its apparent brightness would be immense. Figure 6 shows that if Rigel were as close as Proxima Centauri, then it would be almost as bright as the Moon! Not only would Rigel dominate the night sky, but it would also be clearly visible during the daytime at certain times of the year. The fact that there are no super-giant stars close to the Earth is yet another amazing evidence of design.

(5.5) Ideal brightness of the galaxies

Recent observations with the Hubble Space Telescope have shown that there are at least 50 billion galaxies in the Universe.[2] Some astronomers believe that there could be more than 100 trillion galaxies.[3,4] The average number of stars in each galaxy has been estimated to be at least one billion. If there are at least 50 billion galaxies, and if there are at least one billion stars in each galaxy, this means that there are at least 50 billion billion stars in the Universe. Using figures, this number is 50,000,000,000,000,000,000 stars. If all the stars in the Universe were divided between 5 billion people (the approximate population of the world), then every single person would have at least ten billion stars! Another remarkable feature of the Universe is that every single galaxy, star, planet and moon is unique in size and appearance.

Other galaxies are so far away from the Earth that it is usually only possible to see the combined light of the whole galaxy rather than the light from individual stars. When viewed from the Earth, the sizes of other galaxies are often no bigger than the individual stars that we see in our own galaxy. Galaxies can be recognised because they make fuzzy shapes whereas stars appear as round points of light. The best way to view other galaxies from the Earth is to look in directions where there are not many

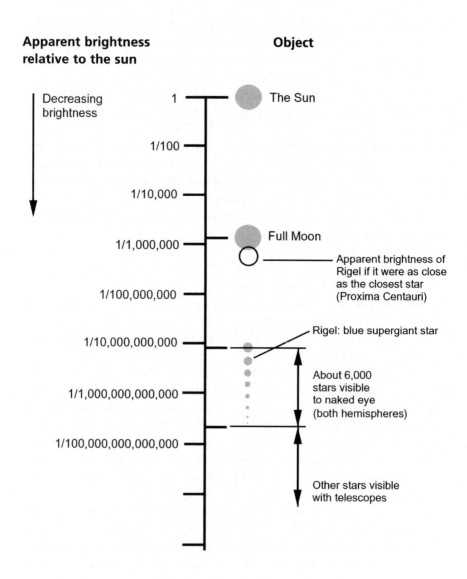

Apparent brightness relative to the sun

Object

Decreasing brightness

1 — The Sun

1/100

1/10,000

1/1,000,000 — Full Moon

Apparent brightness of Rigel if it were as close as the closest star (Proxima Centauri)

1/100,000,000

Rigel: blue supergiant star

1/10,000,000,000

About 6,000 stars visible to naked eye (both hemispheres)

1/1,000,000,000,000

1/100,000,000,000,000

Other stars visible with telescopes

Fig. 6 Apparent brightness of Rigel if it were as close as Proxima Centauri

stars from our own Galaxy. Some galaxies are so big that they can be seen with the naked eye. For example, near the constellation of Pegasus, it is possible to see the Andromeda galaxy (M31) without the use of a telescope. The large Andromeda galaxy is located near to the Milky Way Galaxy and contains the order of 1000 billion stars. With powerful telescopes it is possible to see many millions of galaxies in the night sky.

❶ Right spacing of galaxies

The existence of billions of galaxies represents a brilliant design because galaxies make it possible for the Universe to contain trillions of stars whilst at the same time allowing the Earth's night sky to remain dark. On the one hand, other galaxies are far enough away so as not to be too bright and so that millions of them can be seen in the sky. On the other hand, they are not so far away that we cannot see their fuzzy shape and know that they are galaxies. To illustrate why galaxies are such a good design, it is helpful to consider what would happen if all the stars in the Universe were located in one large galaxy. If all the stars of the Universe were in one large galaxy with the same density of stars as the Milky Way Galaxy, then there would be so much light at night that the whole sky would be as bright as the day.

❷ Understandable hierarchical structure

The number of stars in the Universe is too great to fully comprehend. However, God has put a hierarchical structure in the Universe and this helps man to begin to appreciate the vast number. Our own Milky Way Galaxy teaches us that a Galaxy contains billions of stars. Therefore, when we see other galaxies we know that they too contain billions of stars. The fact that there are many separate galaxies is very useful because it is much easier to count galaxies than count individual stars. To estimate the number of stars in the visible Universe, one can estimate the average number of stars in each galaxy and then multiply this by the estimated number of galaxies. If all the stars in the Universe were in one extremely large galaxy, then it would be very difficult to appreciate the number of stars.

The helpfulness of the hierarchical design of the Universe can be illustrated with the example of viewing an army of a million soldiers. It would be very difficult to comprehend a million soldiers if they were all in one large group. However, if the soldiers were arranged in 1,000 groups, with 1,000 in each group, then the total number could be much better appreciated. This is especially the case if the viewer is within one of the groups of soldiers. In a similar way, God has given us 100 billion stars in our own Galaxy to let us know what a galaxy of stars is like and He has put billions of galaxies at a great distance so that we can estimate the number of other galaxies and the total number of stars.

(5.6) Signs for mankind

Sometimes there are signs in the Solar System that can be seen from the Earth. One of the functions of these signs is to remind people that the stars have a Creator. The most common are planet alignments, comets, meteorite showers, the aurora and eclipses. These events are very striking because the stars normally present a very consistent view from day to day. The signs present an evidence of design because they occur periodically, but not too frequently. On the one hand, if signs happened less than once a century, then most people would hardly be aware of them. On the other hand, if signs happened every day, then they would have little impact. The actual frequency of signs appears to be perfect from a human point of view. In a typical human life-span there will be one or two major signs, like a total eclipse of the Sun or a large comet.

❶ Planet alignments

Planet alignment is caused when two or more planets appear close together in the sky. The main reason for planet alignments is that the planets orbit the Sun in the same plane but at different speeds. As the Earth orbits the Sun, the Earth is overtaking the outer planets but is being overtaken by the inner planets. Since all the planets have different orbital speeds, there are occasions when two or more planets become aligned.

❷ Comets

Comets are bright objects that occasionally move across the sky. They are like large dirty snowballs that occasionally enter the Solar System.

Comets usually have a bright spot and a long tail that fades away. The tail is caused by the effect of heating by the Sun. Most comets pass through the Solar System once and are never seen again. However, some comets have an elliptical orbit and return into the Solar System. Recent comets have included Hale-Bopp and Halley's comet. Comets are very difficult to explain by the Big Bang theory because it is difficult to explain where they come from. According to modern theories, there is an Oort Cloud outside of the Solar System which contains vast numbers of comets. However, there has been no observation of this cloud.

ⓘ Meteor shower

Another special sight in the night sky is that of a meteor shower. One of the most significant showers, called the Perseid meteor shower, occurs on 13th August each year when the Earth passes through the dust of the comet Swift-Tuttle. On the nights near to 13th August, streaks of light (or 'shooting stars') can be seen in the sky. The streaks, which last for a few seconds, are caused by dust heating up and burning due to the friction caused by the dust travelling very fast into the Earth's atmosphere. Other meteor showers occur on 4th January (the Quadrantids), 6th May (Aquarids), 21st October (Orionids) and 14th December (Geminids).

ⓘ The aurora

Another special event in the night sky is that of the 'aurora'. The aurora is a colourful phenomenon that appears over the north and south magnetic poles of the Earth. The aurora is caused by solar wind from the Sun. The solar wind consists of a stream of charged particles and these sweep over the Earth. When the solar wind is strong enough, it interferes significantly with the magnetic field around the Earth and causes charged particles to react with air particles and give off radiation, and it is this which causes the aurora. The aurora is best seen from the most northerly countries like Iceland and Norway but can be seen from many countries further away from the poles.

ⓥ Lunar eclipse

A recent lunar eclipse occurred in Western Europe on the 9th January

2001. A lunar eclipse occurs when the Moon passes into the Earth's shadow so that the Moon is out of direct sunlight. When this happens, the Moon is still lit up because sunlight passes through the Earth's atmosphere and is bent so that it falls onto the Moon. However, as light passes through the Earth's atmosphere it turns red and so makes the Moon red or copper-red. The reason why the reflected light turns red is that the sunlight passes through the extreme edges of the Earth (as viewed from the Sun) and through a long stretch of the Earth's atmosphere as happens at sunset.

ⓥ Solar eclipse

Probably the most famous of special events in the sky is that of a total eclipse of the Sun. This sign event is special because it occurs in the day rather than in the night. A total eclipse is not something that you have to look out for in order to be able to see. Rather, it is something you can-not avoid noticing, unless you are in a windowless building! A total eclipse of the Sun occurs when the Moon passes between the Sun and the Earth. A total eclipse is very striking because the Moon appears the same size as the Sun when viewed from the Earth. In astronomy terms, both the Moon and the Sun make an angle of approximately 32 minutes of arc in the sky. Since the Moon is the same apparent size as the Sun, this means that a total eclipse produces a special 'diamond effect'. If the Moon were at all bigger than the Sun, as viewed from the Earth, then the resulting total eclipse would simply cause a blackout. If the Moon were at all smaller than the Sun, the resulting total eclipse would pro-duce a bright ring that would be too bright to look at with the naked eye. The fact that the Sun and Moon have the same size, as viewed from the Earth, is considered to be just another great coincidence by evolu-tionists. However, a much more logical conclusion is that the size of the Sun and the Moon points towards the existence of a Creator.

5.7 Clocks and calendars for mankind

The Bible teaches that one of the purposes of the stars is to help man know times and seasons. Before the age of modern technology, the Sun,

Moon and stars were a great help to man as a convenient clock and calendar. The stars are still used by creatures such as birds for determining the time of day or night.

The Sun can be used to make quite accurate calculations of the time of day. A sundial makes a shadow on a clock template and can give time to quite a high degree of accuracy, especially when there are separate templates for each month of the year. The stars can be conveniently used to determine the time at night. The reason for this is that the stars appear to rotate around the North Star (in the Northern Hemisphere) and the South Pole (in the Southern Hemisphere) at the rate of one complete revolution per day. By measuring the angle through which the stars have rotated around the North Star or South Pole, an accurate measurement of time can be taken. One of the best ways to find the time in the Northern Hemisphere is to use the pattern of stars referred to as the Plough. This is because the Plough forms a clear pointer towards the North Star.

The Moon is a convenient monthly calendar because its shape in the sky goes through a predictable cycle lasting 29.5 days.[5] Figure 7 shows eight different shapes that can be used to split the Moon's cycle into eight parts. In the Northern Hemisphere, when the Moon is waxing (increasing illumination), the illumination forms on one side to make the letter D, whereas

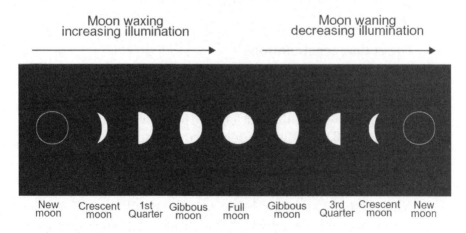

Fig. 7 Phases of the Moon in the Nothern Hemisphere

when the Moon is waning (decreasing illumination), the illumination forms on the other side to make the letter C. If a month is assumed to start with a new Moon, then the first quarter ends when the Moon is a half Moon in the shape of a D, the second quarter ends when there is a full Moon and the third quarter ends when there is a half Moon in the shape of a C. In the Southern Hemisphere, the opposite cycle is seen. Since the Moon cycle has a total period of 29.5 days, the lunar phases of 1st, 2nd, 3rd and 4th quarter last approximately one week which is a convenient time period. In fact, with practice, the exact day of the month can be determined by analysing the size and shape of the Moon. It is amazing that whilst the Moon has an important function of producing the tidal effect, the Moon also performs the function of a calendar system!

The star patterns in the night sky can also be used to determine the approximate date in the year. Since the Earth goes around the Sun, the star patterns change in orientation relative to the Earth. In the Northern Hemisphere, the northern night sky can be seen to rotate anticlockwise by a full circle in the course of one year. In the Southern Hemisphere, the southern night sky can be seen to rotate clockwise through a complete circle. Therefore, by monitoring the orientation of the night sky, it is possible to determine the approximate date in the year.

5.8 The zodiac constellations

In the book of Job we read that God brings out the constellations in their season (Job 38:32). This verse may refer specifically to the twelve zodiac constellations. The zodiac constellations are located approximately around the ecliptic, which is the path followed by the Sun across the sky. The fact that the constellations appear around the ecliptic means that they can be viewed from both the Northern and Southern Hemispheres. It also means that different constellations are visible at different times of year. The Bible teaches that the stars were made for signs and seasons. Therefore, the zodiac constellations may have been made specifically to indicate the seasons of the year. For example, when Gemini is prominent, this indicates that winter has come in the Northern Hemisphere. When Scorpius is prominent, this indicates that summer has come in the Northern Hemisphere.

Some people believe that the 12 zodiac constellations had the additional purpose of explaining the gospel to the early generations of people who lived on the Earth and did not have the Bible. The 12 constellations and their proposed meanings are shown in Table 2. It *may be* that God did use the stars to communicate the message of the gospel to the very early generations of people. However, we cannot be certain about it, so this theory cannot be used as an evidence of design. In addition, it is important that we now rely solely on the Bible for the revelation of God's word and do not seek messages in the stars.

TABLE 2   **THE 12 ZODIAC CONSTELLATIONS AND THEIR POSSIBLE MEANINGS**

CONSTELLATION	PICTURE	MEANING
Aries	Ram	Sacrifice
Taurus	Bull	Resurrection
Gemini	Twins	Christ's dual nature
Cancer	Crab	Gathering of saved
Leo	Lion	King
Virgo	Virgin	Virgin Mary
Libra	Scales	Price of sin
Scorpio	Scorpion	Wages of sin is death
Sagittarius	Archer	Satan
Capricorn	Goat-fish	Earth
Aquarius	Water pourer	Living water
Pisces	Fish	God's remnant

The 12 zodiac constellations are used by astrologers to produce horoscopes. This practice is clearly condemned in the Bible (Isaiah 47:13-14). However, this does not mean that the zodiac constellations are bad in themselves. The problem with astrology is not the existence of the 12 zodiac constellations but the fact that Satan makes people believe that the stars can influence the future.

(5.9) Navigational aids for mankind and creatures

As well as giving the right amount of light on the Earth, the stars also have a very important function as an aid to navigation. They are ideally suited to navigation because they form very distinctive patterns in the night sky. Before the age of technology, stars were used extensively by people for navigation on sea and land journeys. Even though people do not use the stars for this purpose much today, they are still used by many creatures. Studies have shown that some birds use the stars to navigate during night-time flying. A remarkable aspect about bird navigation is that it must be carried out by instinct. Birds have star patterns written onto their genetic code so that when they see stars at night, the sighting stimulates a response in the bird's brain and the bird instinctively moves in a certain direction. This response occurs on the very first occasion that the bird is navigating even though the bird may never have seen the stars before.

(5.10) The star of Bethlehem

A very special case of navigation by stars occurred at the time of the birth of the Lord Jesus Christ. Just after the Lord Jesus was born, the wise men wanted to visit Him in order to bring gifts. However, the wise men did not know that Jesus had been born in Bethlehem. The Bible tells us that the wise men were led by a star as follows:

'and behold, the star which they had seen in the East went before them, till it came and stood over where the young Child was.' (Matthew 2:9)

From this account, it is clear that the star moved through the sky because it 'went before' them and then 'stood' over the place where Jesus was. Therefore, we must conclude that the star of Bethlehem was a supernatural star and not a natural event such as a supernova.

Notes on Chapter 5

1 **Brunier, S,** *Majestic Universe*, Cambridge University Press, p 82, 1999.
2 Ref 1, p 93.
3 One trillion = one thousand billion = 1,000,000,000,000.
4 **Woodward, S,** *Things to come*, Cambridge Alumni Magazine, No 30, p 25, Easter 2000.
5 It may be that the Moon had a cycle of exactly 28 days before the Fall. If this is the case, then the Moon could have been used to signify 7-day weeks after each Moon quarter.

The beauty of the Universe

'By His Spirit He adorned the heavens' (Job 26:13).

The book of Job describes how God has 'adorned the heavens' by His Spirit. Modern telescopes have revealed the astounding degree to which God has indeed adorned the heavens with beauty. When we look up at the stars and galaxies with powerful telescopes, there are countless beautiful colours, shapes and patterns to behold. Whichever direction we look and however far we look, there are sights of outstanding natural beauty. Despite the great evidence of design, secular astronomers totally reject the idea that God has deliberately put beauty in the stars. They do not deny that the stars are beautiful but they insist that the beauty has appeared by chance. This chapter shows that the beauty of the Universe is so striking and so co-ordinated that it provides great evidence of supremely intelligent design.

6.1 The Earth

One of the most beautiful views in the Universe is that of the Earth when looking from space. When astronauts walked on the Moon, they found that they had breathtaking views of the Earth. The Earth is a beautiful oasis in the blackness of space with its beautiful colours of blue, white and green. When looking at the edges of the Earth there is also a beautiful thin atmosphere clinging to the Earth. Another reason for the beauty of the Earth is the way it is lit up by the stars. As Thomas Watson said, 'the heavens were bespangled with the Sun, Moon and stars that so the world's beauty might be beheld and admired.'

6.2 Sunset and sunrise

Sunsets and sunrises can be very beautiful because the sky can be coloured in a mixture of red and yellow shades. The red and yellow colours are produced because of the way white light is scattered. When white light is scattered to a moderate degree, blue is produced because scattering intensity is much greater for colours of a shorter wavelength such as blue. However, when light is scattered to a very high degree, the blue colour is completely removed and a red or yellow colour is produced. During the daytime, the Sun's rays do not have a great distance to travel through the Earth's atmosphere and so there is only a moderate amount of scattering and blue is the dominating colour. However, at sunset and sunrise, the Sun's rays have a greater distance to travel through the Earth's atmosphere. When certain atmospheric conditions exist, this distance can often be enough to turn the sunlight into beautiful red and yellow colours.

6.3 Planets and moons

One of the beautiful aspects of the Solar System is the great variety of colours, shapes and patterns amongst the planets and moons. The planet Mars is commonly known as the 'red planet' because of its red appearance when viewed from the Earth. In contrast, Uranus is green-blue and Saturn is yellow. Some of the moons also have distinctive colours and patterns. Io, one of Jupiter's moons, is known as the 'giant pizza' because of its reddish-brown colour and pizza-like surface. In contrast, Europa, another of Jupiter's moons, is so smooth that it resembles a billiard ball. The Earth's Moon has the added advantage that it is very easy to observe with the naked eye. The way that the Moon makes a different shape every day and changes position produces a beautiful effect. The occasional Moon-glow that is caused with some cloud conditions can be particularly beautiful. There is also a great variety in size in the planets and moons: Jupiter is the largest planet with a diameter of 140 thousand km and Pluto is the smallest planet with a diameter of just two thousand km. The moons also range from the very big to the very small. Ganymede, which is a moon of Jupiter, is bigger than the planet Mercury and almost half the diameter of the Earth. In contrast, some of the moons in the solar system are so small that they have only recently been discovered with powerful telescopes.

One of the most beautiful shapes in the Solar System is the planet Saturn

Fig. 8a Saturn

with its ring system. A picture of Saturn is shown in Figure 8(a). The ring system consists of many separate concentric rings of different colours and these combine to form a gigantic band right around the planet. The neatness of the ring system and the way it fits exactly around the equator of Saturn produces a spectacle of profound beauty.

Perhaps the most famous pattern in the Solar System is the cloudy pattern on the planet Jupiter as shown in Figure 8(b). One of the most striking features on the surface of Jupiter is a dark 'red spot' which is located in the southern hemisphere of the planet. Studies have shown that the red spot is caused by a giant storm. The red spot looks small from the Earth, but it is actually over 10 thousand km in length (similar to the diameter of the Earth) so the spot represents a fantastically large storm. One of the remarkable features of the red spot is that it has been there ever since astronomers first studied the planet 300 years ago. The ability of a giant storm to remain intact for hundreds of years

Fig. 8b Jupiter

has astounded scientists because storms on the Earth last for only a few weeks. According to the Big Bang theory, the red spot on Jupiter and the ring system around Saturn were caused by chance. However, a much better explanation is that they were put there deliberately to make a beautiful and striking effect.

6.4) The Milky Way band of light

The beautiful band of light from the Milky Way can be seen from both the Northern and Southern Hemispheres. The existence of bright city lights and pollution in modern times means that it is often difficult to see the outline of the Milky Way in the night sky. However, on a clear night away from city lights, it is not difficult to observe the Milky Way with the naked eye. This is particularly the case in the Southern Hemisphere where the Milky Way is brightest.

The best time of year to view the Milky Way is around June and July because it is at this time when the constellation of Sagittarius and the centre of the Galaxy is highest in the sky. The best places to view the Milky Way are in the Southern Hemisphere near to the Tropic of Capricorn, (i.e. in countries like Australia, South Africa, Chile and Argentina) because Sagittarius passes right overhead at the end of June. Keen astronomers sometimes make a special trip to an Australian desert at the end of June to get a really clear view of the Milky Way. The best method to appreciate the Milky Way is to lie down on the ground and look upwards, so that the Milky Way can be viewed from one horizon to the other. When this is done the observers have the impression that the Milky Way is right in front of them and there is a stunning three-dimensional view of the Galaxy. The view can be so spectacular that it can stir up deeply emotional feelings in the observer. In fact the view is so breathtaking that people who suffer from vertigo, sometimes have the fear of dropping off the Earth!

6.5) The size and colour of the stars

One reason why stars are beautiful is that they come in a great range of sizes. Right across the night sky there is a great variation in brightness of the stars. The variation in brightness is mentioned in the Bible where we read: 'There is one glory of the Sun, another glory of the Moon, and another glory of the stars; for one star differs from another star in glory.' (1 Corinthians 15:41).

Another reason why the stars are beautiful is that most stars are white-yellow when viewed with the naked eye and this makes a sharp contrast with the black background of space. The ideal white-yellow colour of most stars should not be taken for granted because stars actually come in a range of colours which includes red, yellow, white and blue. There are enough white-yellow stars to create a generally clear contrast with the blackness of space, but there are also enough red and blue stars to give a beautiful variety. Betelgeuse in Orion and Antares in Scorpius are examples of bright red stars that can be seen with the naked eye. Rigel in Orion is an example of a blue star that can be seen with the naked eye.

The colour of a star is determined mainly by its temperature: a red star is relatively cool; a yellow star is slightly hotter; a white star is hotter still; and a blue star is very hot. When God created the stars on the fourth day of creation, He deliberately created each star with a specific temperature that would produce the colour that He wanted. God made the temperature of most stars such that they would give a white-yellow colour.

The fact that stars come in a range of colours is often used by evolutionists as an evidence for the Big Bang theory. By assuming that all stars start off as hot, evolutionists argue that the existence of cooler stars is evidence that the Universe has been cooling for billions of years. However, this reasoning is based on the assumption that all stars started off in the same way. Since there is a clear reason why God would want to create stars with a variety of colours (and hence temperatures), it is wrong to assume that all stars started off life in the same way. In fact, the range of colours that we see today presents great evidence of design.

(6.6) Star patterns

Another reason for the beauty of stars is that they form varied patterns in the sky. Many of the star patterns have been given names such as Great Bear, Little Bear, Cancer and Orion. One of the most striking star patterns in the sky is the Orion constellation. In the Northern Hemisphere, Orion is particularly prominent from December to January. A picture of the Orion constellation is shown in Figure 9. Orion is also referred to as Orion the hunter because it is possible to picture the outline of a hunter with a belt and a sword in the star pattern. One of the reasons for the beauty of Orion is that the stars form quite a geometrical pattern. Another striking feature of Orion is the variety of colours in the stars. The upper left star, called

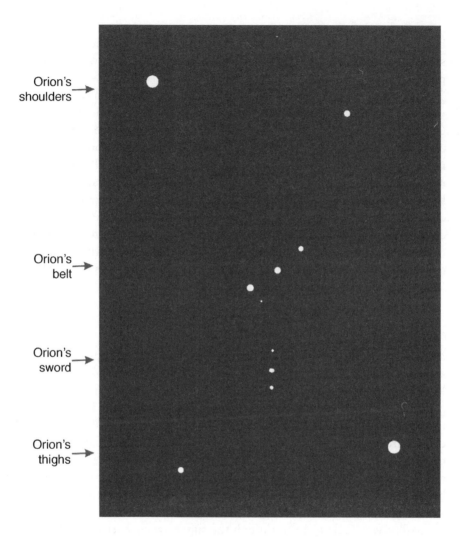

Fig. 9 The Orion Constellation

Betelgeuse, is red whilst the bottom right star is blue. In addition, in the sword of Orion there is the famous Orion nebula, which is coloured red and pink.

Since there are billions of stars in the Milky Way Galaxy, there are virtually an infinite number of patterns that exist in the night sky. The Galaxy is so vast that it is impossible for astronomers to carry out a complete survey of the sky. When a powerful telescope is pointed at the night sky there is always the possibility that a new beautiful sight will be revealed. The Bible teaches that God deliberately made star patterns. In the book of Job we read: 'He made the Bear, Orion, and the Pleiades, and the chambers of the south' (Job 9:9). Not only has God deliberately chosen the colour of each star but He has also chosen the position and size of each star to form beautiful patterns in the night sky. It is amazing to think that the colour, size and position of every one of the billions of stars in the Milky Way Galaxy was determined for the benefit of mankind.

6.7 Special stars

Most stars are of a type called 'main sequence'. An example of a main sequence star is our own Sun. When a main sequence star cools to a certain level, it changes into either a 'red giant' star or a 'white dwarf' star. A red giant is a very large red star that is relatively cool. In contrast, a white dwarf is a very small white star that is relatively hot. Both red giants and white dwarfs are special kinds of stars that can produce quite dramatic effects in the sky. Sometimes a red giant is observed to explode. When this happens, the explosion is called a 'supernova'. A supernova causes an extremely bright light for typically several weeks. On 23 February 1987, a super-giant star exploded in the Large Magellanic cloud which is a satellite galaxy of the Milky Way Galaxy. Even though the supernova occurred way beyond the Galaxy, the supernova was so bright that it could be seen with the naked eye for several weeks. At its maximum brightness, the supernova was several million times brighter than the Sun.

Sometimes a white dwarf sheds material as it contracts and this material forms an enormous expanding shell of gas around the star, called a 'planetary nebula'. The expanding shell of gas is then lit up by the very hot white dwarf. White dwarfs are so hot that they sometimes emit significant amounts of ultraviolet radiation. As visible light and ultraviolet light from the star pass through the shell of gas, the gas is lit up with spectacularly beautiful colours and patterns. One of the most beautiful planetary nebulae in the Galaxy is the Helix Nebula NGC 7293. This nebula consists of a massive bright green inner ring and a large red outer ring. The inner ring contains oxygen gas and the outer ring contains hydrogen gas.

When scientists first discovered planetary nebulae, they were amazed to find the colour green. The reason for this is that stars do not themselves emit any green colours. Scientists were so surprised to find green in space that they thought they had discovered a new material and they even gave the supposed new material the name of nebulium. However, scientists later realised that in certain special conditions, oxygen gas can produce a green colour. According to the Big Bang theory, the spectacular beauty of supernovae and planetary nebulae is just an accident of nature. However, a much better explanation is that they were deliberately designed.

(6.8) Gas and dust clouds

The Milky Way Galaxy contains many gas and dust clouds. Some of these clouds extend for billions of kilometres in space. Gas and dust clouds may not immediately be thought of as very beautiful. However, astronomers sometimes describe gas and dust clouds as some of the most beautiful objects in space. The colour of gas clouds is produced when the light from nearby stars lights up the gas. Since there is a range of gases and stars in space, gas clouds come in a whole range of colours. One of the most famous gas clouds is the Orion Nebula, which can be seen in some detail with binoculars. When viewed with a powerful telescope, the Orion Nebula appears as a fantastic wispy cloud with shades of red and pink. This spectacular gas cloud ripples through millions of kilometres of space with thousands of strands. Brunier describes the Orion Nebula as 'undoubtedly the most beautiful nebula in the sky'.[1]

Dust clouds can also produce very beautiful effects. When a dust cloud is illuminated by a nearby bright star, the light is sometimes scattered to produce huge blue clouds. One such cloud can be found in the border between the constellations of Scorpius and Ophiuchus.[2] The fact that blue is produced in space by the scattering of light is fascinating because this physical process is commonly seen on the Earth. Scattering is used to produce a blue sky, blue feathers in birds, blue wings in butterflies and blue eyes in people.

(6.9) Galaxies

Galaxies come in a number of different shapes including spiral and elliptical. As well as forming beautiful shapes, galaxies can be coloured red or blue. Even though the Milky Way Galaxy is a spiral galaxy, it is difficult to appreciate the shape because we cannot see it from the outside. However, there are many spiral galaxies that can be viewed in the Universe. The best views are those where the spiral galaxy can be seen face-on because this reveals the spiral arms most clearly. One of the most striking spiral galaxies that astronomers have discovered is shown in Figure 10(a). This spiral galaxy is called NGC 6872 and is particularly beautiful because it has two very long arms that extend for many billions of kilometres of space. Each spiral arm contains many billions of stars. The other fuzzy shapes in Figure 10(a) are other galaxies, whilst the points of light are stars within the Milky Way Galaxy. When looking at Figure 10(a) account should be taken that the stars are relatively close by, whereas the galaxies are a very long distance away.

One of the most well known spiral galaxies is the Andromeda galaxy (M31) which is found in the Andromeda constellation. A picture of the Andromeda galaxy is shown in Figure 10(b) (and on the front cover of the book). This is of great interest to astronomers because it is part of the local group of galaxies which includes the Milky Way Galaxy. In addition, the Andromeda galaxy is the largest in the Local Group. When there is a clear moonless night away from city lights, the Andromeda galaxy is easily visible with the naked eye. Astronomers have estimated that the Andromeda galaxy contains more than 1000 billion stars. Since galaxies contain typically billions of stars, there is virtually an infinite variety of shapes that they can have. Since there are billions of galaxies in the Universe, there will always be new shapes to discover.

Fig. 10a Spiral galaxy NGC 6872

Fig. 10b Andromeda galaxy

(6.10) The colour scheme of the Universe

It is very easy to take the colours of the Earth, the sky and the stars for granted. However, in reality the colour scheme of the Universe is amazingly well designed for man. Table 3 summarises the colour scheme of the Universe showing which colours dominate, which colours are secondary and which colours are rare in each part of creation. For clarity, only the primary colours red, green and blue are shown, together with white. For each colour, the most common physical process by which the colour is produced is given.

TABLE 3   **THE COLOUR SCHEME OF THE UNIVERSE**

ENVIRONMENT	DOMINATING COLOUR	SECONDARY COLOURS	RARE COLOURS
NIGHT SKY	BLACK & WHITE	RED, BLUE	GREEN
	(space and starlight)	(starlight)	(oxygen ionisation)
DAY SKY	BLUE	RED	GREEN
	(scattering of light)	(absorption of light)	(aurora)
LAND	GREEN	RED	BLUE
	(chlorophyll)	(plant pigment)	(scattering/ pigment)

One reason why the colour scheme is perfect is that the colours which dominate in each part of creation are 'restful' colours. Studies have shown that green is very easy on the eyes and reduces eyestrain. Blue is a restful colour because it slows down the heart rate. The night sky is also restful because it is so dark. In contrast to these colours, red is quite a stressful colour which raises the blood pressure. If either the land or sky were dominated by red, then life would be very stressful!

A second reason why the colour scheme is perfect is that there is a different dominating colour in each part of creation. The blue sky contrasts with the green land and with the white stars. If the sky and land were both blue or both green, life would be very strange. A third reason why the colour scheme is perfect is that all three primary colours can be seen in each part of creation. Even though red does not appear as a dominating colour in any of the environments, this is made up for by the fact that it appears as a common secondary colour in each case.

A fourth reason why the colour scheme is perfect is that a dominating colour in one environment becomes a rare colour in another environment. For example, blue, which dominates in the sky, is a relatively rare colour in plants and creatures because blue pigments are very rare and scattering of light is not common in plants and animals. The rarity of blue in creatures and plants is ideal because it helps to emphasise the contrast between the land and the sky. A similar situation exists for the colour green. Green, which dominates on the land, is a relatively rare colour in the sky and space. In the sky, green is produced when the solar wind interacts with the Earth's magnetic field to cause the aurora. In space, green is caused when a very hot star ionises an oxygen cloud. The way that green changes from being a very common colour on the Earth to a very rare colour in space is ideal because it emphasises the fact that life exists only on the Earth.

It is very difficult for the Big Bang theory to explain how the entire colour scheme in the Universe could just appear by chance and then happen to be just right. The perfect colour scheme in the Universe presents astounding evidence of design.

(6.11) The philosophy of the Big Bang theory

One of the sad consequences of the Big Bang theory is that it gives no acknowledgement to the Creator for the beauty of the Universe. The most important thing to know about the beautiful Orion nebula is that God created it. And yet God is not acknowledged when astronomers present the Orion nebula. Modern astronomy books present pictures which reveal the beauty of the Universe, but there is always an accompanying message explaining how the beautiful sight must have been produced by chance. Every time a beautiful feature is discovered in space, evolutionists immediately try to think up natural processes that could explain how the feature came into existence by chance.

It is very sad that man looks through telescopes and concludes that the beauty is not there for his sake. Children and students are taught that the colours, shapes and patterns of the Universe are just some side effect of a 'Big Bang'. By denying the origin and purpose of beauty, modern astronomy books and television programmes are leaving out the most important and wonderful facts about the Universe. The truth is that colours, shapes and patterns have been deliberately put in place to produce a beautiful sight and to declare God's glory.

6.12 The purpose of beautiful stars

One of the reasons why God has made the stars beautiful is that He takes joy in His creation (Revelation 4:11 AV). Another reason is that God wants mankind to enjoy the beauty of the stars. The Lord Jesus spoke of beauty in creation when he taught that the lilies of the field were more beautiful than Solomon in all of his glory (Matthew 6:28-29). Nothing that man has made can match God's creation for beauty. This is true not only for the Earth but also for the stars. Job says this about the stars: 'He does great things past finding out, yes, wonders without number' (Job 9:10). Powerful telescopes have demonstrated the profound truth of this verse. In an age when we are surrounded by man-made entertainment, it is important to take time to look up at the stars at night to see how God has 'adorned the heavens'. How we need to follow the advice of Elihu who said: '...stand still and consider the wondrous works of God.' (Job 37:14).

Notes on Chapter 6

1 **Brunier, S,** *Majestic Universe*, Cambridge University Press, p 35, 1999.
2 Ref 1, p 28.

The attributes of God revealed in the stars

'For since the creation of the world His [God's] invisible attributes are clearly seen, being understood by the things that are made, even His eternal power and Godhead, so that they are without excuse' (Romans 1:20).

The Bible teaches that God's invisible attributes have been clearly revealed since the beginning of time and that man has never had an excuse for not believing in a Creator. With powerful telescopes, man now has the advantage that he can see great distances into the Universe and see the attributes of God more clearly than any other generation. John Calvin often spoke of the importance of the revelation of nature. In his *Institutes* he said:

'This is, indeed, the proper business of the whole life, in which men should daily exercise themselves, to consider the infinite goodness, justice, power and wisdom of God, in this magnificent theatre of God.'[1]

7.1 The glory of God

The psalmist tells us that the heavens declare the glory of God (Psalm 19:1). A person or an object can be said to be glorious when they have attributes such as brightness, splendour, beauty and power. When a powerful king is dressed up in bright robes, he can be referred to as a glorious king. This is why the Lord Jesus referred to the glory of King Solomon (Matthew 6:29). Even though earthly kings and queens can be glorious, nothing can compare with the glory of God. Nothing can have greater brightness, splendour, beauty and power than God. The Bible teaches that God's glory is bright (Revelation 21:23, Ezekiel 10:4, Luke 2:9) and brighter than the Sun (Acts 26:13). The Bible also teaches that God is beautiful (Psalm 27:4), powerful (Psalm 147:5) and that He has a glorious majesty (Psalm 145:5).

The Sun, Moon and stars declare the glory of God because they have great brightness, splendour, beauty and power. When we consider the brightness of the Sun, we can be reminded that God's brightness is even more brilliant. When we consider the splendour of the billions of stars and galaxies, we can be reminded that God's splendour is even greater. When we consider the beauty of the colours and patterns in the Universe, we can be reminded that God is even more beautiful. When we observe the greatness of the Universe we can remember that God is greater still. King Solomon described the infinite greatness of God when he said: 'Behold, heaven and the heaven of heavens cannot contain You. How much less this temple which I have built!' (1 Kings 8:27). The Sun and stars show that God is a glorious God who is worthy of our praise. This is why the psalmist said: 'O Lord our Lord, how excellent is Your name in all the Earth, You who set Your glory above the heavens!' (Psalm 8:1).

7.2 The power of God

The prophet Isaiah describes how the stars reveal God's power:

'Lift up your eyes on high, and see who has created these things, who brings out their host by number; He calls them all by name, by the greatness of His might and the strength of His power; not one is missing.' (Isaiah 40:26)

When we think of the billions of stars that exist in the Universe, we can be encouraged that it is by the strength of God's power that none are missing. It does not take much effort to lift one's eyes to the heavens and yet we do this so little in the modern age. How we need to find time to occasionally lift up our eyes to the stars to see what God has created and to consider God's awesome power.

One of the reasons why the stars reveal God's power is because of their immense size and energy. The diameter of the Sun is about 1.4 million km and its mass is about two thousand billion billion billion kg. Put another way, the diameter of the Sun is about 100 times larger than the diameter of the Earth and the mass of the Sun is about 330,000 times greater than the mass of the Earth. The temperature of the Sun is thought to vary from about 15 million K at the centre to 6,000 K at the surface. The enormous size and temperature of the Sun means that it produces an immense amount of energy. Even though the Sun is 150 million km from the Earth, its heat and energy are great enough to be clearly felt.

The incredible size and energy of the Sun are impossible to comprehend with the human mind. But God has created at least 50 billion billion other stars! Since our Sun is considered to be a typical size of star, it is clear that the amount of material and energy in the Universe is absolutely staggering. Since God has created the stars of the entire Universe by speaking them into existence, He must be infinite in power. In addition, the way that God sustains the Universe also demonstrates His awesome power.

When God spoke of His power to Job, He mentioned the stars in the following way:

'Can you bind the cluster of the Pleiades, or loose the belt of Orion? Can you bring out constellations in its season? Or can you guide the Great Bear with its cubs?' (Job 38:31-32)

An interesting aspect of these verses is that Job had already mentioned the Bear, Orion and the Pleiades earlier on in the book of Job (Job 9:9). In Chapter 38 God reminds Job of the star patterns that Job mentioned earlier and uses them to illustrate His omnipotence. Only God could have created the stars of the Pleiades to form a cluster. No one can move the three bright stars that God has put in Orion's belt and only God controls the movement of the Earth so that the position of the stars changes from one season to another.

Seeing God's attribute of power in the stars should be a great encouragement to the Christian because it shows that however difficult our situation is in this life, God is well able to help us. This truth is stated clearly by the prophet Jeremiah:

'Ah, Lord God! Behold, You have made the heavens and the Earth by Your great power and outstretched arm. There is nothing too hard for You' (Jeremiah 32:17).

When we look at the billions upon billions of stars of the Universe, we should remember that all the host of them were made 'by the breath of His mouth' (Psalm 33:6). No wonder the psalmist went on to say: 'Let all the Earth fear the Lord; Let all the inhabitants of the world stand in awe of Him. For He spoke, and it was done; He commanded, and it stood fast' (Psalm 33:8-9).

(7.3) The wisdom of God

The psalmist tells us that the stars reveal God's wisdom:

'Oh give thanks to the Lord…To Him who by wisdom made the heavens' (Psalm 136:3 & 5).

God's wisdom is clearly revealed in the way that the Universe is full of great order and beauty. The psalmist also tells us that God's wisdom is so great that He alone is able to count and name the stars: 'He counts the number of stars; He calls them all by name. Great is our Lord, and mighty in power; His understanding is infinite' (Psalm 147:4-5). Modern studies in astronomy have shown that there are so many stars that it does indeed require infinite understanding to count and name them all. Since man has very limited wisdom it is impossible for man to count and name the stars. Even if man could count at a rate of one million stars a second, it would take at least a million years to count the stars of the Universe! Man's wisdom is so limited that he is unable to even count the number of galaxies in the Universe.

There was a time when secular astronomers thought they could count the galaxies in the Universe. However, this project ended in humiliation for the scientists involved. The history of the project has been described in a secular astronomy book:

'At one time, astronomers had an ambition to catalogue all the galaxies. Charles Messier, Louis XV's astronomer, discovered about sixty, and at the end of the 19th century, the Danish astronomer Johan Dreyer recorded nearly 10,000, after three decades of observations. At the turn of the century, astronomers – who were quite ignorant of the true nature of the small, indistinct patches of light they were finding in the sky – still had no idea of the utter impossibility of the task they had set themselves. Nevertheless, as the power of telescopes increased, so too did the number of galaxies... James Keeler, who studied them with the Crossley 91cm telescope at the Lick Observatory, estimated in 1900 that their total number was slightly more than 100,000. Between the 1950s and 1980s, astronomers at the observatories at Palomar in the Northern Hemisphere and La Silla and Siding Spring in the Southern, commissioned Schmidt telescopes (a form of powerful, wide-field camera), with the aim of mapping the whole sky. The sensitive plates that were obtained were so rich that scanners, linked to powerful computers running shape-recognition software had to be used to make a census of galaxies. Several tens of millions had been recorded on the photographic plates. Since then, no further census of galaxies has been attempted.'[2]

From the above quotation it can be seen that for over one hundred years man pursued the ambition of counting the number of galaxies in the Universe. Over this period, the most powerful telescopes were commissioned and computers were employed to help carry out the counting. Despite these great efforts, the astronomers eventually realised that they could not possibly count the number of galaxies. It is interesting to note in the quotation that Brunier describes how the astronomers had no idea of the 'utter impossibility of the task'.

Astronomers cannot count the number of galaxies in the Universe. And yet counting galaxies is easy in comparison to counting stars! Accounts like this one make one marvel at the stubbornness of modern man. The vastness of the Universe clearly reveals a Creator of infinite wisdom. The inability of man to count the stars should cause him to be humbled and to acknowledge the greatness of the Creator. And yet many still refuse to believe that a Creator exists. One is reminded of the story of Lazarus in which the rich man who died asked Abraham to send Lazarus in order to warn his brothers about the fate of unbelievers (Luke 16:19-31). Jesus pointed out that there were enough warnings in the scriptures already. In a similar way, there are already enough wonders in the Universe to demonstrate clearly that there is a God.

Had astronomers believed what the Bible says about the stars, then they would have realised that it was going to be impossible to carry out a census of galaxies. The Bible teaches that there are so many stars that it is impossible to count them. In the book of Jeremiah we read: 'As the host of heaven cannot be numbered, nor the sand of the sea measured, so will I multiply the descendants of David…' (Jeremiah 33:22). This statement is remarkable because in Bible times it was only possible to count up to about 3000 stars in the night sky. Since 3000 is quite a manageable number to count, biblical writers had to be inspired by God to write that the true number of stars was actually countless.

Seeing God's wisdom in the stars should be an encouragement to the Christian because it shows that God is well able to determine what is best in the life of each Christian. In the same way that God understands each individual star, so He understands each individual life. The Bible teaches that God cares so much for His people that He has even numbered the hairs on their heads (Matthew 10:30).

7.4 The goodness of God

The psalmist described how God is good to all people:

'The Lord is good to all, and His tender mercies are over all His works' (Psalm 145:9).

One way in which the stars reveal God's goodness is demonstrated when we see that the stars help man in practical ways. They provide a calendar, a clock, a navigation system and nightlights. God has also been good to man in the way in which the stars make so many beautiful sights. They show God's goodness in giving a clear testimony to the Creator. God has not hidden Himself from man. The Universe declares that there is a God and that He is a glorious God of infinite power and wisdom. He wants man to see from nature that there is a God and then to read the Bible in order to learn about salvation.

(7.5) The enduring message of the stars

The psalmist describes how the stars declare God's glory day by day:

'The heavens declare the glory of God; and the firmament shows His handiwork. Day unto day utters speech, and night unto night reveals knowledge. There is no speech nor language where their voice is not heard. Their line has gone out through all the Earth, and their words to the end of the world' (Psalm 19:1-4).

Notice how the psalmist says that the stars give out words with their voice. The stars not only shine light on the Earth but they literally 'preach' a message to mankind about the glory of God. It is ironic that at a time when we can see God's attributes more clearly than ever before, there has never been so much atheism in the world. This unbelief bears witness to the great stranglehold that Satan has on the present age. There is now a great need to follow the exhortation of the psalmist who said: 'Proclaim the good news of His salvation from day to day. Declare His glory among the nations, His wonders among all peoples. For the Lord is great and greatly to be praised; He is to be feared above all gods. For all the gods of the peoples are idols, but the Lord made the heavens' (Psalm 96:2-5).

When one understands the incredible power and wisdom of God and the utterly limited nature of human wisdom, it changes the way one views human theories of origins like the Big Bang theory. Should we believe the Genesis account of creation that was inspired by the God who created the heavens and who names all of the stars? Or should we believe man's Big Bang theory when man is unable to even count the number of galaxies? There is a tremendous need for the theologians and church leaders of today to recognise the awesome wisdom of God. Only then will there be the humility to believe the word of God rather than the theories of man.

Notes on Chapter 7

1   Calvin, J, *Genesis*, Banner of Truth, Genesis 1:28, p 105, 1965.
2   Brunier, S, *Majestic Universe*, Cambridge University Press, p 93, 1999.

PART II
THE QUESTION OF
EXTRATERRESTRIAL
LIFE

A historical overview of man's belief in extraterrestrial life

'The fool has said in his heart, "There is no God"'
(Psalm 14:1).

The phrase 'extraterrestrial life' is a term used to describe the physical life that secular scientists believe exists on planets other than the Earth. History shows that people's interest in extraterrestrial life is closely linked with atheism and belief in the theory of evolution. The logical consequence of belief in evolution is the belief that life can spontaneously arise anywhere where conditions happen to be right. Since the Universe contains many billions of stars, evolutionists believe that there must be life elsewhere in the Universe. History also shows that science fiction has had a major influence on popular belief in aliens.

8.1 Pre-Copernicus (circa 4000 BC to AD 1500)
Before Nicolas Copernicus (AD 1473-1543) made his discoveries about the Solar System there was no significant interest or belief in extraterrestrial life. There were two main reasons for this. One reason was that early Christians ruled out the possibility of extraterrestrial life on the basis of biblical doctrines. The second reason was that the Greek philosopher Aristotle taught

that the Earth was at the geographical centre of the Universe and was therefore a unique planet.

Biblical doctrines had an important influence on the beliefs of people in many parts of the world before AD 1500. The early Christian writers taught that biblical revelation about the creation of the Earth and the redemption of mankind meant that the Earth was a unique life-bearing planet. For example, in his book *City of God*, Augustine (AD 354-430) used these biblical doctrines to argue that there were no other worlds.[1] Christian writers also considered belief in a plurality of worlds an atheistic idea.

Greek philosophers also had a major influence on the beliefs of many people until AD 1500. Some of the Greek philosophers such as Democritus (460–c.370 BC) believed that there could possibly be other worlds. However, the more influential teacher Aristotle (384-322 BC) was convinced that the Earth was the only world in the Universe. Aristotle believed that the Earth was the geographical centre of the Universe and, therefore, the Earth was unique as a life-bearing planet. In his treatise *De Caelo*, Aristotle argued strongly against other worlds using the analogy that just as a circle has one centre, so the Universe can have only one centre if it is to be an ordered whole.[2] After the time of Aristotle, the Greek geographer Ptolemy (AD 127-151) produced maps of the Universe showing the Earth to be at the centre. These maps were accepted as a true representation of the Universe until around AD 1500. It is important to emphasise that early Christians rejected extraterrestrial life not because of the teaching of Aristotle but because of the teaching of the Bible.

8.2 Copernicus to Darwin (1500 – 1859)

Around AD 1500, there was a revolution in astronomy when Copernicus discovered that the Earth went around the Sun, not the Sun around the Earth. Galileo also played a key role in showing the true nature of the Solar System. The discovery of the Solar System showed that Aristotle was wrong to think that the Earth was the geographical centre of the Universe.[3] The additional discovery that there were other planets orbiting the Sun further emphasised that the Earth was not geographically unique.

The discovery that the Earth was not at the geographical centre of the Universe was entirely consistent with biblical teaching about the uniqueness of the Earth. The Bible teaches that the Earth is at the centre of God's purposes, not that the Earth is at the geographical centre of the Universe. Therefore, the discovery of Copernicus did not change the Christian view that there could be no extraterrestrial life. The great majority of reformed Christians still believed that, from a biblical point of view, there could be no extraterrestrial life. For example, in the sixteenth century, the Lutheran reformer Philip Melanchthon (1497-1560) argued that life on Earth was unique. In his *Initia Doctrina Physica* (1567), he wrote that life on other planets was ruled out because of the doctrine of the once-and-for-all redemptive work of Christ.

However, the discovery of Copernicus did change the thinking of non-Christians. Before AD 1500, non-Christians generally followed the teaching of Aristotle that the Earth was unique and there could be no aliens. However, after AD 1500, non-Christians believed that the Earth was not unique and the question of the possibility of other worlds was seriously debated. However, there was still no popular interest in aliens because there was no explanation as to why aliens should be on other planets.

(8.3) Darwin to the present age (1859 to present)

In the late nineteenth century there was a tremendous birth of interest in extraterrestrial life. There is no doubt that Darwin's theory of evolution was the catalyst for this interest. In 1859 Charles Darwin published his *Origin of Species* which proposed that life had evolved gradually on the Earth over millions of years by chance. One of the consequences of Darwin's theory of evolution was that there was suddenly an explanation of how life could appear on other planets. As the theory of evolution became accepted in the late nineteenth century, there was a great rise in interest in extraterrestrial life.

Early interest in extraterrestrial life focused on the possibility of life on the planet Mars. There were two main reasons for this. Firstly, Mars was known to orbit the Sun at a distance that is not too dissimilar to that of the Earth. This feature gave evolutionists a reason to believe that Mars could possibly have the right climate for life to evolve. Secondly, Mars was close enough for detailed observations to be made using the telescopes of the time. The Italian astronomer Giovanni Schiaparelli made some of the first detailed observations of Mars' surface in 1877 when he observed what seemed to be a network of canal-like features on Mars. At first, there were no claims that these canals had been produced by an intelligent life-form. However, in 1894 an American called Percival Lowell produced a theory proposing that the canals were artificial and built for a purpose. In 1894 Lowell wrote:

'Here we have a reason for the canals. In the absence of spring rains a system of irrigation seems an absolute necessity for Mars if the planet is to support any life upon its great continental areas.'[4]

Lowell's theory quickly became very popular and had widespread appeal. For nearly two decades many people really thought that there was intelligent life on Mars. Only in 1909 did an astronomer, Antoniadi, show that the canals were actually an optical illusion caused by shading of surface features. The fact that people believed for so long that artificial canals existed on Mars shows how easy it is to convince people that there is extraterrestrial life. Even though close observations showed no sign of intelligent activity on Mars, there was still a strong belief amongst scientists that there was living vegetation on Mars. For example, in 1928 there was a symposium for the public in the USA about life on Mars and this was entitled *Eminent Astronomers Give Their Reasons for Their Belief that Life exists on the Great Red Planet.*

Another significant increase in interest in extraterrestrial life came during the 1930s when Edwin Hubble and others proposed the Big Bang theory. According to this theory, the Universe has evolved over billions of years following a Big Bang. Whereas Darwin's theory of biological evolution attempts to explain how people could have evolved from lifeless chemicals, the Big Bang theory attempts to explain how the Earth could have evolved from a single crude explosion of matter. The 1930s marked a significant point in human history when people attempted to describe how the entire Universe could have evolved from a single crude event. According to the Big Bang theory, many Earth-like planets could have evolved by chance elsewhere in the Universe. Since this theory was first proposed, the majority of people, including most scientists, have believed that there is some kind of life elsewhere in the Universe.

Another important factor that has influenced modern belief in extraterrestrial life is the discovery that the Universe contains a vast number of stars. During the twentieth century, the estimated number of stars continually increased because of the use of increasingly powerful telescopes. Even during the 1990s, the estimated number of stars in the Universe went up following observations by the Hubble Space Telescope. During the twentieth century, estimations of the number of galaxies in the Universe steadily grew from a few thousand to a few million to a few billion. Some astronomers now think there may be as many as one hundred trillion galaxies in the Universe. The discovery of vast numbers of stars has caused many evolutionists to claim that there must be life elsewhere in the Universe.

The widespread current belief in extraterrestrial life can be seen in many ways. Firstly, governments are prepared to spend billions of dollars to pay for spacecraft and telescopes that are dedicated to searching for extraterrestrial life. Secondly, the idea that there is such life is beginning to play a serious part in the education system. For example, in 1999 the first 'Professor of Extraterrestrial Life' was appointed at the University of California at Berkeley, USA. Thirdly, extraterrestrial life plays a major role in science fiction.

(8.4) The rise of science fiction

There is no doubt that science fiction stories and films have helped to reinforce the general belief that there is alien life in space. Before the end of the nineteenth century, aliens did not appear in fictional literature. However, following the acceptance of the theory of evolution and the resulting popular belief in alien life, aliens quickly started to play a big part in fictional stories. The use of alien life made such a dramatic impact on fiction that a separate branch of fiction known as 'science fiction' (or 'sci fi' as it sometimes known) was quickly born. During the twentieth century there was a steady rise in popularity of science fiction.

Historians are in full agreement that the inspiration behind science fiction was the theory of evolution and that its key element has always been extraterrestrial life. Steven Dick, who is a leading expert in this field, has said:

'It is a remarkable fact of history that only in the last third of the 19th century did extraterrestrials enter the realm of literature...the birth of alien literature is closely tied to late 20th century science, especially evolutionary theory...During the 20th century the concept of the alien became a leitmotif of the young genre known as 'science fiction'...' [5]

The first popular science fiction story was *War of the Worlds* by HG Wells (1866-1946), which was first published in book form in 1898. The story line in *War of the Worlds* was that life had evolved by chance on Mars and that Martian life was more advanced than life on Earth. The reason for the superiority of the Martians was that theirs was a smaller planet and would therefore have cooled more quickly than the Earth, thus facilitating an earlier start to evolution than was possible on Earth. The superiority of the Martians meant that they could monitor the Earth in a way that humans could not monitor Mars. It also meant that they could travel through space to the Earth whereas humans could not yet travel in space. In *War of the Worlds*, the Earth received a surprise invasion of Martians and this led to a fierce battle.

Wells was inspired to create alien beings in his science fiction after embracing Darwin's theory of evolution. As well as being influenced by Darwin, HG Wells was almost certainly influenced by Percival Lowell who popularised the Martian canal theory. Steven Dick said this about Wells:

'Wells was a man of his time in many ways, not least because of his championship of Darwin's theory of evolution. As Fechner was Lasswitz's great influence, the biologist TH Huxley was Wells'. Huxley, the 19th century's greatest champion of Darwinian evolution, taught Wells from about 1883 to 1886 at the Normal School of Science in London. Huxley's evolutionary viewpoint is pervasive in Wells' early writings in science and science fiction, and it forms the broad background to the advanced beings in the War of the Worlds.' [6]

At the beginning of the twentieth century, HG Wells was the most popular author, with stories like *War of the Worlds, The Time Machine* and *The Wonderful Visit. War of the Worlds* was so popular that it was serialised for radio by Orson Welles in 1938. It was during one of these broadcasts that some listeners were sent into a panic about a possible real invasion from Mars. The radio broadcast included a fictitious news bulletin that Martians were actually invading the Earth, and this bulletin was taken seriously by many people. The resulting panic became a famous incident in radio broadcasting history.

Another big boost in science fiction popularity came in the 1960s with the advent of the space age. With man planning space travel to the Moon, the interest in science fiction suddenly grew to great proportions. Some of the major science fiction films and series are listed in Table 4.

TABLE 4 **MAJOR SCIENCE FICTION FILMS AND TELEVISION SERIES**

DATE	TITLE
1960s	Star Trek series
1960s	Dr Who series
1968	2001: A Space Odyssey (Arthur C Clarke)
1977	Star Wars
1977	Close Encounters of the Third Kind
1979	Alien
1980	The Empire Strikes Back
1982	ET: The Extra Terrestrial
1983	Return of the Jedi
1986	Aliens
1987	Star Trek: The Next Generation
1992	Alien III
1996	Independence Day
1997	Alien Resurrection

As well as these films, there have been eight *Star Trek* feature films from 1979 to 1996. Also, a new series of *Star Wars* films has recently been started. Science fiction films are now so popular that they often have the biggest box office appeal of all types of films, making billions of dollars in profit. The number of people who have seen *Star Wars* or *Star Trek* films is so large it would be easier to count the number of people who have not seen them. There is no doubt that films like *Star Trek* and *Star Wars* have a great influence on people's belief in extraterrestrial life. When young children are brought up on such films, it is not surprising that they develop a deep belief that aliens do exist.

Notes on Chapter 8

1 **Augustine**, City of God, XI, 5.
2 **Aristotle**, De Caelo, I, 8, 277a.
3 Since we do not have a fixed reference point outside the Universe, we do not actually know where the centre of the Universe is. Some people argue that even though the Earth goes around the Sun, the Earth could still conceivably be at the exact centre of the Universe. However, what is certain is that from the frame of reference of the known Universe, the Earth is not at the exact geographical centre.
4 **Dick, SJ,** *Life on Other Worlds*, Cambridge University Press, p 33, 1998.
5 Ref 3, p 107.
6 Ref 3, p 112.

The importance of extraterrestrial life to present day society

'Professing to be wise, they became fools'
(Romans 1:22).

In the present age, many scientists believe that science has replaced religion by providing answers to questions such as origins and the meaning of life. Many scientists also believe that only science can save the human race from extinction. The question of whether there is extraterrestrial life is considered to be one of the most important questions to be addressed in the twenty-first century. Scientists think that the discovery of such life would finally provide convincing evidence for the theory of evolution. Many people also think that extraterrestrial life holds the key to understanding the meaning of all life and possibly even saving the human race from extinction.

9.1 The search for evidence of evolution

The truth about origins has vital implications for what happens after death. If God has created the Universe, then it follows that man is a special being and that there is life after death and a day of judgement. However, if God has not created the Universe, then it follows that there is no life after death. Considering the profound importance of origins, it is not surprising that people want to prove which theory of origins is correct. A great problem with Darwin's theory of evolution is that there is no evidence that evolution has taken place on the Earth. Some of the main problems with the theory of evolution are:

❶ No evidence of pre-biotic evolution in the laboratory

Evolutionists believe that 'simple life' arose spontaneously from a primordial soup that is believed to have existed in the early history of the Earth. To demonstrate the feasibility of this event, evolutionists have tried very hard to replicate the spontaneous generation of life in the laboratory. However, there has been no success. Evolutionists often claim that Miller's experiment in 1953 was successful because he produced the basic building blocks of organic matter. However, these experiments never came close to making a self-replicating living organism. The fact that scientists cannot replicate the spontaneous generation of life, even with the help of modern equipment, provides very strong evidence that life has never spontaneously appeared in the past.

❷ No evidence of evolution of new types of creatures

There is not a single example of a fundamentally new type of creature that has been seen to evolve despite attempts to accelerate the process of evolution either by selective breeding or by induced genetic mutations. Examples of subspecies coming from a single species have been observed, but this has never produced a fundamentally new kind of creature. For example, it is possible to breed unusual horses but it is not possible to change a horse into another kind of creature like a giraffe. Also, no genetic mistakes have been discovered that have led to any increase in genetic information. Creatures are observed to be decaying in design rather than progressing. This decay is entirely consistent with the second law of thermodynamics.

❸ No evidence of evolution in the fossil record

The fossil record does not contain intermediate types of creature between the main classes of creature we see today. For example, there is nothing to connect birds with other types of creature. Only birds have feathers, and feathers are irreducibly complex. Even fossils of the most unusual extinct birds, like Archaeopteryx, show feathers that are identical to those of modern flying birds. Many evolutionists fully admit that the fossil record does not support gradualistic theories of evolution. For example, the Harvard palaeontologist George Gaylord Simpson has said:

'It is a feature of the known fossil record that most taxa appear abruptly. They are not, as a rule, led up to by a sequence of almost imperceptibly changing forerunners such as Darwin believed should be usual in evolution.'[1]

ⓥ The Design Argument

The design argument states that where there is design, there must be a Designer. Probably the most serious problem with the theory of evolution is that the Universe bears the hallmarks of a Supreme Designer. The design argument in relation to life on Earth is summarised in the book *Hallmarks of Design*.[2]

The lack of evidence of evolution on the Earth has led many scientists to believe that the search for extraterrestrial life is now one of the most important ways of obtaining evidence for evolution. If evidence of extinct micro-organisms were to be found on a planet like Mars, then this would be seen as evidence that life had spontaneously evolved on that planet in the past. Also, if primitive life used to exist on Mars, then this would be seen as evidence that such life could have existed on the Earth in the past. This is why NASA and other institutions that promote evolution are so keen to find evidence of fossil life on Mars.

NASA has always seen a close link between evolution and extraterrestrial life. On the official NASA web site, NASA includes in its vision for the future:

'NASA's Space Science activities seek to answer fundamental questions concerning the galaxy and the Universe; the connection between the Sun, Earth and heliosphere; the origin and evolution of planetary systems; and, the origin and distribution of life in the Universe…Space Science continues to focus on fundamental questions regarding the creation of the Universe … and the possibility of life beyond the Earth.'[3]

The importance of extraterrestrial life to evolutionists has been described by Jakosky:

'Finding non-terrestrial life would be the final act in the change in our view of how life on Earth fits into the larger perspective of the Universe. We would have to realise that life on Earth was not a special occurrence, that the Universe and all of the events within it were natural consequences of physical and chemical laws, and that humans are the result of a long series of random events... The discovery of life elsewhere would have an effect... on the views of fundamentalists. For the same reason that they do not accept that evolution occurred on the Earth, the existence of life on other planets and the possibility that that life could evolve would threaten their views...'4

Scientists will never be able to find real evidence for evolution on the Earth because evolution has never occurred. Therefore, it is likely that the search for extraterrestrial life will be carried out vigorously by the scientific community for many years to come and probably until the end of the world.

9.2 The search for the meaning of life

To non-Christians, the search for extraterrestrial life is closely linked to the search for the meaning of life. In the same way that Christians look to the Bible for answers to ultimate questions, evolutionists look to the Earth and stars to obtain the answers to ultimate questions. The recent book *Life on Other Worlds*, published by Cambridge University Press, has a dedication to those who are 'searching for the meaning of life'. The book also has a major chapter entitled 'The meaning of life'. The importance of the search for extraterrestrial life is often summed up in the following popular quotation:

'There are two possibilities. Maybe we're alone. Maybe we're not. Both are equally frightening.'5

Even established scientific bodies are eager to relate the search for extraterrestrial life to the search for the meaning of life. In a report by the Space Science Board of the National Academy of Sciences in the USA in 1962, the following statement was made:

'It is not since Darwin... that science has had the opportunity for so great an impact on man's understanding of man. The scientific question at stake in exobiology [evolution of life outside the Earth] is, in the opinion of many, the most exciting, challenging, and profound issue, not only of this century but of the whole naturalistic movement that has characterised the history of Western thought for three hundred years. What is at stake is the chance to gain a new perspective on man's place in nature, a new level of discussion on the meaning and nature of life.'[6]

Notice how there is a close link here between evolution, Western thinking, extraterrestrial life and a search for the meaning of life. This link is still present in the space programmes of the American space agency NASA. The main reason that extraterrestrial life is linked to the meaning of life is that atheistic philosophy is unable to provide any answers to the ultimate questions of life. Atheism cannot explain why the Universe exists and what the future holds. The only way that atheism can attempt to answer such questions is by looking beyond the Earth in the hope of finding other habitable worlds.

According to atheistic philosophy, man will one day become extinct and it will be as if man had never existed. This is why the logical conclusion of atheism is that life on Earth is ultimately pointless unless mankind can emigrate to other planets or at least make contact with other life-forms. Atheists believe that the most noble aim of the human race is to perpetuate human life in the Universe for as long as possible and to communicate with other life forms if at all possible. If mankind could communicate with other intelligent life before extinction comes, then at least other beings would have been told that there used to be life on the Earth.

(9.3) The salvation of the human race

The search for extraterrestrial life is not only linked closely with the meaning of life, but it is also linked with the salvation of the human race. According to atheistic philosophy, the biggest problem for the human race is that life on Earth could be destroyed by a large meteorite impact, or an ice age, or even by a period of global warming. Even if there is not a natural catastrophe that wipes out life on Earth, there is still the problem that the Earth will run out of resources or the Sun will eventually run out of fuel and not be able to heat the Earth.

Some scientists believe that the discovery of extraterrestrial life would help to provide an escape route for mankind. It is thought that the search for life in space could help in a number of different ways:

i Another more advanced intelligent life form might communicate with us and teach us how to emigrate to other habitable planets.

ii Another more advanced intelligent life form might come and rescue us.

iii The study of a potentially habitable planet such as Mars teaches us about the nature of the planet and helps us to plan for creating a habitable climate on Mars.

The belief that extraterrestrial life could help to save the human race is one of the reasons for the popular interest in science fiction films such as *Star Trek* and *Star Wars*. In such films, people are often saved from catastrophe by the skills and bravery of space travellers. Many people believe that NASA and other space agencies have the potential skill and power to save the human race. This is one reason why governments are prepared to spend billions of dollars on the search for life in space.

The belief in the potential role of extraterrestrial life in human salvation is also the reason for the large growth in new religions that include a significant space or alien dimension. For example, in many New Age religions, it is believed that it is possible to make mystical contact with aliens. A popular book on UFOs published in 1990 says this about extraterrestrial life and salvation:

'People are increasingly looking to extraterrestrial life as a means for salvation.'7

There is also a growing trend for people to believe that they are related to aliens. A great many people in the West believe in some form of reincarnation. Many of these people even believe that they have been reincarnated from life on other planets. Some people also point to the Big Bang theory to argue that they are related to aliens. According to this theory, all the materials of the Earth, including the materials in the human body, were previously part of the stars in the Milky Way Galaxy. This leads some people to think that they are related to life elsewhere in the Universe. The author Brad Steiger published a popular book in 1981 called *Star Birth* in which he said:

'Right now all over the world, certain men and women are responding to some remarkable internal stimulus…They are having peculiar memories surface which remind them that their true ancestral home is a very distant, a very alien "somewhere else".'[8]

Notes on Chapter 9

1 **Simpson, GG,** *The history of life*, in Vol. 1 of Evolution After Darwin, University of Chicago Press, 1960.

2 **Burgess, SC,** *Hallmarks of Design*, Day One Publications, Epsom, Surrey, 2000.

3 NASA website.

4 **Jakosky, B,** *The Search for Life on Other Planets*, Cambridge University Press, p 301, 1998.

5 Ref 4, p 1.

6 **Dick, SJ,** *Life on Other Worlds*, Cambridge University Press, p 238, 1998.

7 *UFOs The Continuing Enigma*, Dorling Kindersley Book, London, p 106, 1992.

8 Ref 7, p 206.

The search for extraterrestrial life

'There is none who understands; there is none who seeks after God' (Romans 3:11).

There is a desperate need in the modern age for people to seek after God. One of the ironies today is that man would much rather seek after extraterrestrial life than seek God. When NASA claimed that a fossil rock from Mars had been found in August 1996, there were headlines in the media around the world. Many European newspapers devoted almost entire front-page coverage to the news. How sad that man should have so much interest in a little rock and so little interest in the Creator of the Universe who came to Earth 2000 years ago.

(10.1) Funding the search for extraterrestrial life

Scientists are interested in searching for both intelligent and non-intelligent extraterrestrial life. Evolutionists believe that other planets could contain life of varying degrees of evolution. They believe that some planets may contain nothing more complex than microbial life and others may contain nothing more complex than vegetation. In cases where scientists are searching for intelligent extraterrestrial life, the search is often referred to as SETI (Search for ExtraTerrestrial Intelligence).

Governments all over the world contribute very large sums of money to support space missions and astronomy projects that are directly related to searching for evidence of life in space. The annual space budget for NASA is of the order of $15 billion. A significant proportion of this money is spent directly on searches for extraterrestrial life. For example, NASA has sent a total 13 spacecraft to the planet Mars and each one has cost between $100 million and $1 billion. The primary aim of these spacecraft has been to search for signs of life either directly or indirectly. Private companies also donate large sums of money towards such projects. Recently, Microsoft donated $12.5 million towards a SETI project.[1]

10.2 Unidentified Flying Objects (UFOs)

Most scientists now consider the possibility of alien visits to the Earth as extremely unlikely in the short term. There are two main reasons for this. Firstly, the distance between our Solar System and its nearest star neighbours is too great for any aliens to be able to travel to the Earth. The nearest star to our Solar System, Proxima Centauri, is 40 thousand billion km away. Even if aliens happened to live on this nearest star, and could build a spaceship that could travel at a colossal one million km per hour, they would still take over 4,500 years to get to the Earth! Secondly, it would be much easier for aliens to communicate with us by radio signals than to travel to us. Since no signals have been detected, it is assumed that aliens do not live on nearby planets. Even though the existence of alien spacecraft around the Earth is considered to be very unlikely in the short term, it is useful to consider the history of UFO sightings because this shows that there was a time when scientists did take them seriously.

One of the first publicised sightings of a UFO came in 1947 when an American pilot, Kenneth Arnold, claimed he saw several strange disc-shaped objects flying in formation whilst he was flying his private aircraft. The American Air Force thought that UFOs could pose a security threat to American airspace, whether they were from the Soviet Union or from outer space. Therefore, the American Air Force investigated sightings of UFOs through projects 'Sign' and 'Grudge', which were started in 1948. Members of the public were encouraged to report sightings of UFOs to the American Air Force and the sightings were formally recorded. It was in 1952 that the American Air Force coined the phrase 'Unidentified Flying Objects' (UFOs). In 1952, previous projects were superseded by the American Airforce's project 'Blue Book' which ran until 1969. Throughout each year of the Blue Book project there were hundreds of reported sightings. The sightings attracted a lot of media attention and many people believed that aliens were really visiting the

Earth. The total number of sightings recorded by the American Air Force from 1948 to 1969 totalled over 10,000. The American Air Force decided to produce an official report of the UFO sightings which was to be conducted by senior scientists. The report was called the Condon Report and was officially delivered to the American Air Force in 1969. The report was nearly 1,000 pages long and it concluded that there was no firm evidence that any of the sightings were extraterrestrial in origin. However, the report stated that there was always the possibility of a visit from aliens in the future![2]

In the present age there is still a great interest in UFOs with a large number of clubs and magazines on the subject. Many people are still convinced that aliens really do visit the Earth. A related subject to UFOs is that of unidentified markings on land, such as crop circles. In many countries, including the UK, farmers have reported strange patterns appearing in their crop fields. These patterns are caused by the flattening of specific areas of the fields to form an indented pattern. The appearance of crop circles has caused some people to think that aliens are landing in fields at night.

There are a number of different explanations for the sightings of UFOs. One of the most common is that people have simply seen a man-made aircraft. It is no coincidence that the increase in civil air traffic in the second half of the twentieth century in the USA coincided exactly with the increase in UFO sightings. During this period there were probably also spy aircraft sent by the Soviet Union to cross Europe and the USA. These flying machines would have been particularly likely to fall into the UFO category because their presence would have been unexpected.

Another explanation for UFOs is that of natural phenomena like astronomical events or adverse weather conditions. In 1972 there was a UFO sighting in France by a reputable family who reported three bright round airships in close formation. However, it was discovered that on the particular night in question there was a close alignment of three planets (Venus, Jupiter and Saturn) and this alignment fully accounted for the sighting.[3] There are also natural explanations for crop circles. For example, scientists have found that wind turbulence can account for some of the patterns that have been reported. Sometimes UFO sightings are the result of deliberate hoaxes and some people have confessed to making up UFO stories. There is also very strong evidence that the vast majority of crop circles have been man-made.

Even though misinterpretations and hoaxes can explain the vast majority of UFO sightings, it is possible that there are some UFOs that cannot be explained this way. It is quite possible that some UFOs could be the work of satanic forces. There are many people in the current age who practice witchcraft and sorcery. When people experiment with witchcraft, it is possible that satanic signs appear. Some Christian authors have also seen a link between the end times and the increase in UFO sightings.[4]

(10.3) Mars

The search for life on other planets in the Solar System accounts for the most ambitious and expensive projects in the search for extraterrestrial life. Interplanetary spacecraft have travelled to all of the planets in the Solar System apart from Pluto. In some cases, the spacecraft have gone right to the surface of the planet, as with Venus, Mars and Jupiter. In other cases, the spacecraft have flown near to the planet and taken close-up pictures. One of the main aims of these planetary missions has been to look for signs of life. There are three main ingredients that evolutionists believe are required to evolve life: (i) liquid water; (ii) biogenic materials; and (iii) energy. Biogenic materials are defined as the basic chemicals that make up organic materials. These basic chemicals include carbon, hydrogen, oxygen and nitrogen. Examples of energy include chemical, light, lightning and heat. Scientists believe that Mars and Europa (a moon of Jupiter) have these three ingredients now or at least have had them in the past. Therefore, many space missions are being directed at Mars and Europa.

One of the first priorities of the space age was to send a spacecraft to the surface of Mars in order to look for evidence of life. The Americans were the first to reach Mars with two Viking spacecraft in 1976. This mission is reported to have cost around a billion dollars, which was a vast sum of money at that time. When the two Viking spacecraft landed on Mars, they carried out a series of eight separate surface experiments to determine whether there was life. Most experiments were looking for evidence of metabolic activities of micro-organisms. All the experiments had negative results. However, even some of the scientists involved in the Viking projects still refuse to accept that the evidence collected by the Viking spacecraft proved that there were no living creatures on Mars.

In the last 15 years there have been several missions to Mars. One of the most important missions after the Viking missions was the 'Mars Pathfinder' spacecraft that landed on Mars on July 4, 1997. The spacecraft had a rover vehicle called 'Sojourner' which travelled small distances around the Martian surface. This rover made an analysis of the composition of the surface material which again showed no signs of any past or present life. The Mars Pathfinder spacecraft also took a number of panoramic photographs of the Martian surface showing the planet to be dry, rocky and barren.

There are many space projects planned for Mars in the next ten years. Spacecraft are usually sent to Mars during a 'launch window' that occurs approximately once every two years. The reason for the two-year cycle is that the orbital period of the planet Mars is such that it passes close to the Earth approximately once every two years. By launching spacecraft when Mars and the Earth are closest to each other, the time of travel is greatly minimised. The main aim of most of the Mars projects is to search for evidence of life. Some of the major projects are:

❶ Advanced rovers (NASA)
NASA plans to send two robotic vehicles (rovers) to Mars in 2003 at a cost of approximately $600 million.⁵ If successful, these rovers will be able to travel up to 100 metres a day on the surface of Mars, which is further than the Sojourner travelled in its whole lifetime. The rovers will take pictures of the Martian surface and carry out analysis of rocks and soil. One of the main goals of the mission is to determine whether Mars once contained water. NASA believes that if there is evidence of past water, then this supports the idea that there was once life on Mars.

❷ Mars Express Spacecraft (ESA)
In 2003 the European Space Agency (ESA) plans to send the Mars Express spacecraft to Mars at a cost of several hundred million pounds. This spacecraft will orbit Mars and take very detailed three-dimensional pictures.

ⅲ Beagle 2 (UK)

Britain plans to send a spacecraft, called Beagle 2, to Mars in 2003. The little spacecraft will be carried on the Mars Express spacecraft. The mission will cost about £30 million, and its main aim is to 'search for alien life on Mars'.[6] The spacecraft is named after 'The Beagle' which was the ship on which Charles Darwin travelled on his famous trip to the Galapagos Islands. The fact that Beagle 2 is so named shows how scientists see extraterrestrial life as being a very important evidence of evolution.

ⅳ Mars retriever (NASA)

NASA has plans to send a spacecraft to Mars around the year 2005 which will be capable of collecting rocks and bringing them back to Earth. This mission will probably cost several billion dollars because of the complexity involved in launching a spacecraft from the planet Mars to the Earth.

10.4 Meteorites from Mars

Every day, many meteorites from space crash into the Earth. Most meteorites burn up in the atmosphere, but some are large enough to fall as rocks to the ground. Most meteorites are rocks that have originated from space. However, it is possible that a small number of meteorites originate from planets such as Mars. When a large meteorite hits a planet like Mars, the collision could theoretically cause lumps of material from the planet to fly into space and become meteorites themselves. It is also theoretically possible that such meteorites could crash into the Earth. To determine the origin of a meteorite, scientists carry out an analysis of its chemical composition and this is compared with the composition that is thought to exist on other planets in the Solar System. So far, scientists have found about 12 meteorites whose origin is thought to be the planet Mars.

Meteorites that are thought to have originated from other planets provide scientists with the opportunity to carry out thorough examinations to test for evidence of past life. NASA and other scientific institutions now search extensively for meteorites in case they show evidence of coming from other planets. One of the most common searching sites is the

Antarctic because any meteorites found there are generally uncontaminated by Earth-based materials. Another advantage of Antarctica is that meteorites are usually dark in colour and are therefore easy to find on the white snow.

In August 1996 there were world headlines when NASA claimed to have found a Martian rock with evidence of fossil life in worm-like cavities. The rock was found in Antarctica and given the number ALH 84001. The cavities were thought to be fossil evidence of primitive life on Mars. Scientists believed that the meteorite was 4.5 billion years old, of a period when Mars is thought to have had an atmosphere and possibly water. It was hypothesised that a meteorite impact fractured the rock about 3.6 billion years ago and that another impact 16 million years ago, launched the rock into space where it eventually intercepted the Earth. The press release showed that the NASA team were very confident about the evidence. They said that there were four pieces of evidence that 'when taken together provided convincing evidence of past life on Mars'. However, when more detailed tests were carried out on the rocks, the general consensus amongst scientists was that the worm-like holes were not fossils at all but just empty cavities. Nevertheless, even to this day, NASA still insists that the ALH 84001 meteorite may contain real fossil evidence. As with the Mars canal theory, the Mars rock shows how willing scientists are to believe that there has been life on Mars.

(10.5) Europa

Many scientists believe that Europa, one of the moons of Jupiter, may have contained life in the past and may even be supporting life now. The reason for this is that Europa contains abundant water in the form of a thick layer of ice which surrounds the moon. Even though the water around Europa is in the form of ice now, it is thought that in the distant past the temperature of Europa could have been high enough for the water to exist at the surface in a liquid state. Even now it is possible that there is a liquid water mantle beneath the ice surface of Europa. Since liquid water is one of the most important substances required for life, it is thought that life may have spontaneously evolved on Europa in the past. Some scientists even believe that it is possible that life still exists under the ice at the present time. The possibility of finding life on Europa is being taken so seriously that great efforts are being made not to contaminate the planet with false evidence of life. For example, the Galileo spacecraft, which is due to orbit Jupiter until 2002, is planned to be dumped into the Jupiter surface to ensure that it does not crash into Europa.

10.6 Planets around other stars

The search for planets around other stars represents a very important activity in the search for extraterrestrial life. There are a number of reasons for this. Firstly, if many other planets can be discovered around other stars, this could be used by evolutionists to argue that the Earth is not special. Secondly, if it can be shown that the Universe contains many millions of planets, then it could be argued that there is a high probability that life has evolved somewhere else in the Universe. Thirdly, if scientists can find an Earth-like planet, then this planet will be monitored closely for possible messages from aliens.

The probability of life existing elsewhere is usually estimated by an equation called the 'Drake' equation. This was proposed in 1961 when the American National Academy of Sciences sponsored a meeting about extra-terrestrial life. According to the Drake equation, a certain proportion of stars have planets; a certain proportion of these planets just happen to have the right conditions for life; a certain proportion just happen to have sponta-neously produced primitive life; and a certain proportion just happen to have evolved intelligent life. Evolutionists argue for a high probability of life elsewhere in the Universe by quoting the following statistic: if only one in a million stars has planets, and if only one in a million of these planets has the right conditions for life, and if only one in a million of these planets has evolved life, then there would still be thousands of life-bearing planets in the Universe. By counting the number of planets in a substantial part of the Milky Way Galaxy, scientists aim to estimate the number of planets in the whole Universe and then use the Drake equation to estimate the number of possible life-bearing planets.

The detection of planets outside of the Solar System has only been possible in the last few years. The vast distances to the stars mean that it is very difficult to observe planets directly even with the most powerful telescopes. However, astronomers have developed several techniques for detecting planets. One of the ways in which they are detected is by observing whether a star wobbles. When a star wobbles, this provides evidence that one or more planets are orbiting the star. By August 2000 the number of planets discovered in the Universe had reached 51.[7] Of these, two planetary systems have been discovered which contain more than one planet. According to some reports, the discovery of 51 planets in our vicinity of the Milky Way Galaxy has 'raised the prospect that alien life may be found to exist'.[8] However, all the planets detected so far seem to be very unsuitable for supporting life. The reason for this is that they are gas giants with elliptical orbits.

There are some big projects planned for locating planets outside our own Solar System. Some of these projects will cost billions of dollars. In 2002 the European Space Agency (ESA) will launch a French-built space telescope called Corot. This will attempt to analyse 50,000 stars in order to survey the number of planets. In the longer term, NASA and ESA plan the Terrestrial Planet Finder and Darwin missions in order to survey millions of stars. These missions hope to use space interferometers 50 m in diameter.[9] Such instruments would be able to detect Earth-sized planets even in the distant parts of the Galaxy. The use of Darwin's name in a mission to find planets shows again that belief in alien life is closely linked with the theory of evolution.

(10.7) Searching for messages from space

Another method of searching for extraterrestrial life involves listening for messages from space using radio telescopes. During the early part of the twentieth century, it was discovered that stars and other celestial objects radiate radio waves as well as visible colours. This discovery led to the idea that electromagnetic radiation, such as radio waves, could be used for communicating with extraterrestrial intelligence. Since communication signals can be sent to other stars quite easily, it is thought that signals are the most likely way that extraterrestrial intelligence could be detected. Since 1960, various projects have been carried out to try to contact intelligent life in space. Most projects have involved analysing radio waves or optical pulses from space to search for evidence of intelligent signals. However, some projects have involved sending out signals towards other stars.

In 1967 there was a brief spell of excitement amongst astronomers when someone discovered a pulsing signal from a star in the Milky Way Galaxy. The signal had such a uniform frequency that it was first thought that the signal could be a message from aliens. The signal was even given the code LGM for Little Green Men! However, after some time it was realised that the signal came from a pulsar star. This is a fast rotating star and the pulsating signal is caused by the star's rotation. The Galaxy is now known to contain many pulsar stars.

In 1976 the attempts to establish communication contact with extraterrestrial life were labelled SETI (Search for Extra Terrestrial Intelligence). There is now a SETI institute which funds and co-ordinates global efforts to communicate with extraterrestrial life. The idea of the SETI programme is that telescopes from across the world will carry out a co-ordinated effort to scan the entire sky for alien communications. So far, SETI scientists have used huge radio telescopes to scan a few hundred stars a year. One of the problems with SETI is that it takes a lot of computer processing to analyse the radio waves from space to determine whether there are intelligent patterns. For this reason, a programme has been initiated which allows millions of home PCs from around the world to link into the SETI institute to help carry out the analysis. The PCs are only made to work when the screen saver is operating so that the PC owner does not have to give up any time on the PC. So far, millions of people have voluntarily linked their home PCs to the SETI programme to help with the analysis of signals from space. Despite vast amounts of searching and analysis, astronomers have found no evidence of signals from aliens.

(10.8) Sending messages into space

In many spacecraft and astronomy projects, opportunities are often taken to send messages into space to try to contact intelligent alien life. In each case, a great deal of thought goes into what information to include in the message and how to make the message understandable. Some of the first messages for aliens were written in 1972 and sent with the two Pioneer spacecraft, Pioneer 10 and 11, which were launched in 1972 and 1973 respectively. These spacecraft visited Jupiter and Saturn and have travelled on to leave our Solar System. Pioneer 10 is now outside the Solar System and moving towards the constellation Taurus at the rate of 360 million km per year. Pioneer 11 is heading towards the centre of our Galaxy in the direction of the constellation Sagittarius. Both of these spacecraft have gold-coated aluminium plaques with diagrams explaining where the craft originated from and showing male and female humans.

Messages were also placed on the Voyager 1 and Voyager 2 spacecraft that were launched in 1977. These spacecraft have visited Jupiter, Saturn, Uranus and Neptune and are now heading away from the Solar System. Each Voyager spacecraft has a message inscribed on a gold-plated copper disc like a gramophone record. Attached to the disc is a needle for playing the record. When the record is played, there are 90 minutes of music, 115 analogue pictures, greetings in 60 languages and other natural Earth sounds. The record has an aluminium cover which is designed to keep the record intact for 100 million years!

Another way of sending messages into space is to broadcast radio waves using powerful transmitters. The message shown in Figure 11 was broadcast in 1974 from a gigantic radio telescope at the Arecibo Observatory in Puerto Rico towards the globular star cluster M13. The message was broadcast as a string of 'ones' and 'noughts' but the digital message can be reconstructed into the picture shown. The message gives a few simple facts about humanity and its knowledge. For example, the Solar System is depicted by a column of rectangles with the Sun at the top and the nine planets underneath. Notice how the relative size of the rectangles corresponds with the relative size of the planets. For example, Jupiter and Saturn, the fifth and sixth planets furthest from the Sun respectively, are represented by the largest rectangles. Also, notice how the third planet is the only one on the left side of the column. This is to signify that the Earth is the only planet that contains intelligent life.

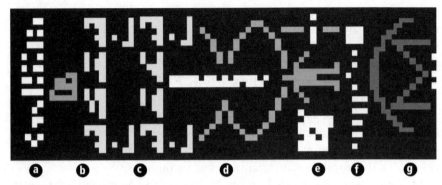

Fig. 11 Message sent out to extraterrestrial life in 1974

KEY

ⓐ numbers from 1 to 10
ⓑ atoms including hydrogen and carbon
ⓒ some interesting molecules
ⓓ human DNA
ⓔ human being with description
ⓕ planets in the Solar System
ⓖ details of sending telescope

Notes on Chapter 10

1 New Scientist, 5 August, p 19, 2000.
2 **Dick, SJ,** *Life on Other Worlds*, Cambridge University Press, p 156, 1998.
3 *UFOs The Continuing Enigma*, Dorling Kindersley Book, London, p 124, 1992.
4 **Larson, B,** *UFOs and the Alien Agenda,* Nelson, pp 193-211, 1997.
5 Report in The Times, 12 August, p 9, 2000.
6 Report in The Daily Telegraph, 7 December, p 11, 2000.
7 Announcement at the International Astronomical Union Conference, Manchester, 7 August, 2000.
8 Report in The Daily Telegraph, 7 August, 2000.
9 **Brunier, S,** *Majestic Universe*, Cambridge University Press, p 74, 1999.

Biblical reasons why there is no extraterrestrial life

'The heavens, even the heavens are the Lord's; but the Earth He has given to the children of men' (Psalm 115:16).

Many people wonder whether there could be extraterrestrial life. The Bible gives a clear answer: only the Earth has been formed to be inhabited (Isaiah 45:18) and the main purpose of the stars is to shine light on the Earth (Genesis 1:17). Therefore we can be certain that there is no extraterrestrial life. Whilst there is no physical life outside of the Earth, it is important to state that the Bible teaches that there are 'spiritual' beings outside of the Earth such as angels. Therefore, we can also say with certainty that there is 'spiritual life' outside of the Earth. In this chapter, the term 'extraterrestrial life' refers only to physical life. This chapter presents eight biblical reasons why there is definitely no extraterrestrial life. It also presents biblical reasons why there are other planets in the Solar System and beyond.

11.1 The importance of the question of extraterrestrial life

In recent years several evangelical authors have been open-minded about the possibility of extraterrestrial life.[1,2,3] However, other authors have stated that extraterrestrial life is definitely not a possibility.[4] Some Christians may be tempted to say that we should be open-minded about the possibility of extraterrestrial life. Others may argue that it is not central to the Gospel message. But both of these arguments are wrong. The question of extraterrestrial life has major consequences on the witness of the Gospel. At best, the search for such life presents an enormous distraction that hinders people from searching the Bible for answers to the questions of life. At worst, it leads to belief in evolution and even mystical religious beliefs. There is a great need today to encourage people to stop searching the Universe for the answers to life and to look to the God of the Bible.

(11.2) Biblical reasons why there is no intelligent extraterrestrial life

Intelligent life is defined as a living being that has the capability of thinking and communicating in an intelligent way. There are at least four specific biblical reasons why there cannot be intelligent extraterrestrial life.

❶ The fall of man (Genesis 3:17-18)

In Genesis 3 we read that Adam and Eve rebelled against God and sinned in the Garden of Eden. As a punishment for this sin, God put a curse on creation as follows: 'Then to Adam He said "...Cursed is the ground for your sake; in toil you shall eat of it all the days of your life. Both thorns and thistles it shall bring forth for you..."' (Genesis 3:17-18).

When Adam and Eve sinned, the whole creation was cursed. There is no part of the physical Universe that has not been affected by the Fall. The universal scope of the curse is described in Romans 8:22, Hebrews 1:11, Psalm 102:26 and Isaiah 34:4. In the case of creatures and plants, the judgement involved ageing, illness and mortality. God's curse on creation shows that mankind is at the centre of God's purposes and that the whole Universe is affected by the actions of mankind. If there were other intelligent beings, then they would also be affected by the Fall. But it would not make sense for other intelligent beings to be condemned because of mankind's actions. Therefore, the Earth-centred nature of God's curse shows that there can be no intelligent extraterrestrial life.

❷ The redemption of man (John 3:16)

Another reason why there can be no intelligent extraterrestrial life is that God has given a special salvation to human beings. In the Gospel of John we read: 'For God so loved the world that He gave His only begotten Son that whosoever believes in Him should not perish but have everlasting life' (John 3:16). Notice in this verse how God loved 'the' world. God does not love many worlds with many different types of physical beings. God has not sent His Son to other worlds to save other beings. Also, the death of Jesus Christ on the cross was a unique, one-off event. In Romans we read: 'knowing that Christ, having been raised from the dead, dies no more. Death no longer has dominion over Him. For the death that He died, He died to sin once for all...' (Romans 6:9-10). If God had made other worlds with intelligent beings, then Christ would have had to die again to save those other beings because the whole Universe has been affected by the Fall. Since Christ's sacrifice was once and for all, we can conclude that there are no other worlds.

One theologian has argued that Christ's death on the cross on the Earth could atone for the sins of beings on other planets.5 This theologian claims that Colossians 1:15-20 can be interpreted as Christ reconciling beings from the entire Universe. However, the Bible clearly teaches that Christ's sacrifice cannot help people who have not heard the Gospel (Romans 10:14). Therefore, it is inconceivable that Colossians 1:15-20 supports the existence of aliens. From the doctrine of redemption, we can conclude that there can be no intelligent extraterrestrial life.

ⅲ The person of the Lord Jesus Christ (Philippians 2:6-8)

The Bible teaches that the Lord Jesus Christ is the Son of God and that He took on the form of a man (Philippians 2:6-8). The fact that the Lord Jesus took on the form of a man shows that human beings are special in the Universe. The Lord Jesus has not taken on the form of any alien life.

ⅳ The pre-eminence of mankind in creation (Genesis 1:26)

Man has a special status in creation because he is the only creature to have been made in the image of God (Genesis 1:26). One of the consequences of being made in the image of God is that mankind is made to have dominion over God's creation. This is described in Psalm 8: 'When I consider Your heavens, the work of Your fingers, the moon and the stars, which You have ordained, What is man that You are mindful of him? ...You have made him to have dominion over the works of Your hands; You have put all things under his feet...O Lord, our Lord, how excellent is Your name in all the Earth!' (Psalm 8:3-9). Notice from these verses that God has put 'all' things under man's feet. If there were alien life elsewhere in the Universe, then man would not have dominion over creation and all things would not be under his feet. The consequence of the teaching of Psalm 8 is that there can be no other intelligent life in space.

(11.3) Biblical reasons why there is no non-intelligent extraterrestrial life

Non-intelligent life is defined as any type of non-intelligent creature or plant or microbial life. There are at least four specific biblical reasons why there cannot be non-intelligent extraterrestrial life:

❶ The purpose of the Earth (Isaiah 45:18)

The way that the Earth was specially prepared over the first three days of creation to support life shows that it is unique as a life-bearing planet. The unique life-bearing function of the Earth is stated in Isaiah: 'For thus says the Lord who created the heavens, who is God, who formed the Earth and made it, who has formed it to be inhabited.' (Isaiah 45:18). All the other planets and stars in the Universe were made on the fourth day and this day was not given to making preparations for life on them. In Genesis 2:2 we read that God rested from 'all' His work which He had done. The clear implication here is that Genesis 1 has described all the work that God had done. Since Genesis 1 does not describe the creation of extra-terrestrial life, we can be confident that there is none in existence.

❶ The pre-eminence of mankind in creation (Genesis 1:26)

From the creation account, it is clear that God made all things for man's sake. John Calvin said this about Genesis 1:

'God Himself has shown by the order of creation that He created all things for man's sake.'[6]

If there were microbial life or vegetation on Mars, this would be useless to mankind. Therefore, we can conclude that there are no kinds of physical life on other planets.

ⓘ The purpose of the stars (Genesis 1:17)

Another reason why there can be no extraterrestrial life is that the stars have a clear purpose of serving the Earth. In Genesis 1:15 and 1:17 we read that the Sun, Moon and stars were all made to 'give light on the Earth'. The Earth-centred purpose of the stars is also stated in Deuteronomy: 'The Sun, the Moon, and the stars…God has given to all the peoples under the whole heaven as a heritage.' (Deuteronomy 4:19). Even the stars in distant galaxies exist in order to shine light on the Earth. The fact that the Sun, Moon and stars were all made after the Earth shows that they have a purpose of serving the Earth. The lower status of the stars compared with the Earth is summed up in the phrase 'He made the stars also'. After a builder has completed a family home, we might say 'he made the gardens also'. In a similar way, the Bible describes the creation of the stars as a secondary matter in comparison to the creation of the Earth. The contrasting purpose of the Earth and the stars is summarised in Psalm 115: 'The heavens, even the heavens are the Lord's; but the Earth He has given to the children of men' (Psalm 115:16). The clear implication here again is that the Earth is unique as a life-bearing planet.

ⓘ The redemption of the Earth and the stars (Isaiah 65:17)

Another reason why there can be no extraterrestrial life is because of the redemption of the Earth. The Bible declares that there will one day be new heavens and a new Earth: 'For behold, I create new heavens and a new Earth' (Isaiah 65:17). This teaching is very significant because it once again highlights the central importance of the Earth compared to the stars. After this world has ended, there will be 'new heavens and a new Earth' in which the Earth will have a central role. Since the Earth will have a central role in the future, it follows that the Earth has a central role at present. The timing of the redemption of the Earth also precludes the possibility of extraterrestrial life. If there were more than one intelligent life form needing salvation in the Universe, then there would be the problem of deciding when to bring an end to the Universe. But there is no such problem because the Earth is the only place to contain life. The central importance of the Earth in the end-times is also described in the Gospel of Matthew: 'the stars will fall from heaven' (Matthew 24:29). This verse again describes the dependence of the stars on the activities on the Earth.

(11.4) Biblical reasons why there are other planets in the Solar System

The Earth is one of nine planets in the Solar System. Evolutionists claim that the existence of other planets in the Solar System provides evidence that Christians are wrong in believing the Earth to be special. This reasoning is sometimes referred to as the 'Copernicus Principle' because it was Copernicus who discovered that the Earth was not the geographical centre of the Universe. However, this reasoning is wrong because Genesis 1 teaches that the Earth is at the centre of God's purposes and not at the geographical centre of the Universe. The existence of other planets in the Solar System does not change the fact that the Earth is special. In fact, there are several important biblical reasons why God created other planets in the Solar System:

❶ To shine light on the Earth (Genesis 1:17)

The fact that all the other planets in the Solar System can be observed from the Earth demonstrates that other planets perform the function of shining light on the Earth. This function, which is stated in Genesis 1:17, would be enough to justify the existence of planets. However, planets have a further function in that they shine light on the Earth in a way that differs to the stars. Planets appear as lights that move relative to the stars and this creates a striking effect in the night sky. Also, the planets vary in brightness depending on how close they are to the Earth. The planets Venus and Mercury are particularly different to the stars because they can appear very bright near to sunset and sunrise when the stars cannot be seen.

❷ To reveal the Creator (Romans 1:20)

As well as shining light on the Earth, the other planets in the Solar System serve the additional purpose of revealing the invisible attributes of the Creator. The other planets in the Solar System contain shapes and patterns that are not seen in the stars and so they add to the revelation of the stars. The rings of Saturn and the cloudy patterns on Jupiter are two particularly striking features of the planets.

ⓘ To give pleasure to mankind (Job 37:14)
In the book of Job we read the exhortation concerning God's creation: '…Stand still and consider the wondrous works of God' (Job 37:14). The other planets represent wondrous works of God and therefore can be appreciated by man.

ⓘ To give pleasure to God (Revelation 4:11)
The Bible teaches that God takes pleasure in His creation (Revelation 4:11 AV).

(11.5) Biblical reasons why there are other planets outside of the Solar System
Very recent observations have shown that some nearby stars have planets around them. Since there are trillions of stars in the Universe, it follows that there could be many millions of planets in the Universe. Evolutionists claim that the existence of planets outside of the Solar System gives particular evidence that the Earth is not special. They argue that if God had created the Universe for mankind, then it would be totally unnecessary for Him to create distant planets because they are completely invisible to the naked eye. The reasoning of the evolutionist is again wrong because there are still several important biblical reasons why God would create distant planets:

❶ To shine light on the Earth (Genesis 1:17)
The fact that it is possible to detect planets outside of the Solar System means that such planets affect the way that light and radiation falls on the Earth and, therefore, it can be said that they perform a function of helping to shine light on the Earth. For example, the fact that a planet causes the parent star to appear to wobble, means that it has affected the way that light shines on the Earth.

⦿ To reveal the Creator (Romans 1:20)

The fact that there are trillions of stars in the Universe reveals the almighty power and wisdom of God. The recent discovery that there are probably many millions of planets in the Universe shows that God's work in creation is even more powerful and wonderful than was previously thought.

⦿ To give pleasure to mankind (Job 37:14)

Discovering new objects in the sky is a fascinating and enjoyable activity. There are so many different objects in the night sky that there is always something new to find. The discovery of other planets has added to the excitement of astronomy and to the wonder of the Universe.

⦿ To give pleasure to God (Revelation 4:11)

Many evolutionists ask the question: Why would God want to create many millions of planets when only a small fraction can be detected from the Earth? One answer to this question is that God takes pleasure in His creation whether mankind is able to see that part of creation or not. Another answer is that since people now know of their probable existence, they can now give God the glory for them.

⦿ To show the uniqueness of the Solar System (Isaiah 45:18)

The planetary systems outside of the Solar System help to demonstrate its wonderful uniqueness. Observations of planets outside the Solar System have revealed very crude planetary systems. Also, there have been no discoveries of Earth-like planets.

⦿ To show the infinite understanding of God (Psalm 147:4-5)

The probable existence of millions of distant planets shows that only God has infinite understanding. The existence of distant unobservable planets teaches man that there are many things that exist in the Universe that will never be seen by mankind. These include distant stars and galaxies as well as creatures and plants on the Earth that people have never discovered. The fact that we know that there is much we cannot see is quite instructive because it emphasises the fact that God alone knows all things.

Notes on Chapter 11

1   **Philpott, K,** *A death blow to Christianity?*, Evangelical Times, April 2000.

2   **Jefferson Davis, J,** *Search for extraterrestrial intelligence and the Christian doctrine of redemption*, Science and Christian Belief, Vol. 9, No 1, pp 21-34, 1997.

3   **Byl, J,** *God and Cosmos*, Banner of Truth, p 125, 2001.

4   **MacKay, T,** *Ten reasons why God made the stars*, Evangelical Times, November 1999.

5   Ref 2, p 30.

6   **Calvin, J,** *Institutes of the Christian Religion 1*, Westminster, Chapter 14, pp 181-182, 1960.

A critique of science fiction

'Do not love the world or the things in the world'
(1 John 1:15).

It is important to state at the outset that there is nothing inherently wrong with fiction as a form of entertainment or education. God has made people with the capacity to be creative in producing fictional stories and films. God has also made people with the need and capacity for recreation in body and mind. Reading a fictional book or watching a fictional film can be an effective form of relaxation and enjoyment. Fiction can also be effective as an educational tool and can even be used to promote godly behaviour. Some of the most well known fictional stories are actually authored by Christians. Indeed, one of the most popular books ever written was John Bunyan's *Pilgrim's Progress*, which is entirely fictional. More recently, the author Patricia St John has written many fictional stories and some of these, such as *Treasures of the Snow*, have been very successful.

12.1 Fundamental principles relating to entertainment

As with ordinary fiction, there is nothing inherently wrong with the concept of 'science fiction'. However, much of science fiction that is currently produced is unsuitable for Christians because it undermines important biblical doctrines in the areas of creation, salvation and supernatural powers. In particular, the portrayal of a Universe with numerous types of intelligent aliens undermines important biblical teaching on the uniqueness of man.

Some people might find it strange to label much of science fiction as unsuitable since so much is classified as mainstream family entertainment by secular society. However, the world hates the teaching of the Bible and so it should be no surprise that much worldly entertainment is ungodly. From the Bible it is abundantly clear that Christians must be very cautious about worldly entertainment. The Bible instructs us not to love the world or the things in the world (1 John 1:15). The Lord Jesus said that what is highly esteemed amongst men is an abomination in the sight of God (Luke 16:15).

The dangers of science fiction have recently been pointed out by Larson:

'While many mums and dads probably pay little attention to the current UFO craze, their children and grandchildren most likely do... movies and television programmes... cannot be dismissed as benign entertainment, or just the latest Hollywood fad. The possibility exists that these media influences will seriously alter a young person's spiritual outlook. Parents need to explain that movies like the Star Wars trilogy were deliberately concocted with a mystical view of reality, and that concepts like 'The Force' are based on metaphysical interpretations of good and evil and are therefore anti-biblical.'[1]

It is very important for Christians to be aware of the dangers that are present in science fiction films such as *Star Wars* and *ET: Extraterrestrial*. In particular, when young children are constantly exposed to science fiction over a long period of time, there is a very real risk of them developing a false view of both the created world and the spiritual world.

(12.2) Biblical doctrines that are undermined by science fiction

There are five biblical doctrines that are particularly undermined by many science fiction stories and films:

❶ The unique spiritual status of man (Genesis 1:27)

The Bible teaches that man is the only creature made in the image of God (Genesis 1:27). The Bible also teaches that human beings are the only physical creatures that have a soul which lives for eternity. From these teachings it is clear that mankind is a unique creature who is at the centre of God's purposes in the Universe. A major problem with many science fiction stories is the inclusion of aliens who are intelligent and spiritual. When this happens, people are given the impression that mankind is not at the centre of God's purposes in the Universe.

ⓘ The unique stewardship status of mankind (Genesis 1:26)

The Bible teaches that man has the unique status of being the sole steward over creation. For example, in Genesis 1:26 we read that man was given dominion over all creation. Also, in Psalm 8:5-6 we read that God has crowned man with 'glory and honour' and that God has put 'all things under his feet'. A major problem with science fiction is that it often includes aliens that are comparable or superior in power to mankind, so that mankind is not portrayed as the sole steward of creation.

ⓘ Biblical teaching on witchcraft (Leviticus 19:26 & 31)

By definition, supernatural powers can only come with the aid of beings from the spiritual realm. Ultimately, the source of supernatural powers is either God or Satan. The practice of exercising supernatural powers that have come from Satan is referred to as witchcraft or black magic or sorcery. The Bible condemns witchcraft as evil (Leviticus 19:26 & 31, Galations 5:20). A major problem with many science fiction films is that aliens are often portrayed as practitioners of witchcraft. In addition, the films portray black magic as a normal activity and this can tempt readers/viewers to try it out for themselves or at least to condone the practice.

ⓘ The universal nature of sin (Romans 3:23)

The Bible teaches that every single person is a sinner in the sight of God (Romans 3:23). It also teaches that only Jesus Christ is perfect. A problem with many science fiction stories is that there is a stereotype in them that many people are either completely good or completely bad.

ⓥ The doctrine of Christ the only Saviour (Acts 4:12)

The Bible teaches that there is 'no other name under heaven given among men by which we must be saved' except the Lord Jesus Christ (Acts 4:12). According to many science fiction stories, there are superheroes around the Universe who are able to save mankind and the Earth from destruction. Sometimes it is human superheroes who are able to save the human race. Either way, such science fiction undermines the biblical truth that only God can save. God makes a warning about the coming of false christs (Matthew 24:24). Therefore, it is important to be wary of false saviours in science fiction.

(12.3) The undermining of the witness of creation (Romans 1:20)

The created world reveals the invisible attributes of God (Romans 1:20). When people are presented with a distorted view of creation, there is a danger that God's attributes are no longer clearly seen. In the same way that people should use a faithful translation of the Bible, so people should become familiar with a faithful picture of creation. A major problem with science fiction is that it often distorts creation through the invention of other planets and other beings. A particular problem is the invention of intelligent aliens who share some of the characteristics of man. God has deliberately made man to have unique physical characteristics to enable him to rule creation and to give him a particularly wonderful beauty. The Bible speaks of the special physical design of man in Psalm 139:14 and throughout the book of the Song of Solomon. When science fiction uses aliens who possess some of the unique characteristics of man, this hinders people from seeing the uniqueness of man and the wonder of the human body. There are four particular characteristics that are unique to man but which are 'borrowed' by science fiction characters:

❶ Unique intellectual capacity

The unique intellectual capacity of humans is no doubt the main reason why they are able to rule creation. The human brain is widely acknowledged as being the most complicated structure known anywhere in the Universe. The human brain has as many as 100 billion neurons and an even higher number of connections between these neurons. This vast system of cells enables a fantastic speed and capacity of intellectual activity and creativity. Animals have fine senses, reflexes and instincts but have no ability to think and create as humans do. When science fiction includes aliens with highly intelligent minds, it is distorting God's creation and detracting from the wonder of the human intellect.

ⓘ Uniquely sophisticated speech

Humans are capable of speaking or singing a given word in a myriad different ways. The fact that there are thousands of languages, each with thousands of words, shows the great range of sounds that are possible with the human voice. In comparison, the vocal utterances of animals are very basic and they can communicate only in limited ways. When science fiction films include *aliens* who can speak as humans do, this again distorts God's creation.

ⓘ Unique upright stature

The unique upright stature of humans is another key reason why they are able to rule creation. Man is a biped (two-legged) whereas other land mammals are generally quadrupeds (four-legged). Even monkeys and apes cannot stand upright properly and cannot walk or run any distance on two feet because they do not have joints for an upright stature and they do not have feet for walking. Walking upright has the advantage that the arms and hands can be dedicated to intricate and creative tasks. The fact that there are thousands of different types of creatures on the Earth that have a horizontal stature provides great evidence that humans have been deliberately designed to be masters of creation and to be unique. The significance of the upright stature of man has been pointed out by the Bible commentator Matthew Henry:

'Man has this advantage above the beasts, in the structure of his body, that whereas they are made to look downwards, as their spirits must go, he is made erect, to look upwards, because upwards his spirit must shortly go and his thoughts should now rise.'[2]

When aliens are presented as standing like man there is the danger that human beings are no longer considered as being uniquely upright.

ⓘ Uniquely agile hands

Humans have uniquely agile hands that enable them to carry out complex and creative tasks. In the case of animals, all of their limbs are designed for very specific tasks such as locomotion, fighting and eating. In the case of humans, the hands and fingers are designed for delicate and controlled movement to enable them to perform a multiplicity of tasks. In particular, humans have very delicate skin that enables the fingers to carry out precision tasks. Human beings can perform amazing levels of controlled movement with their hands in writing, music, medicine, art, building, sport and almost every area of activity that distinguishes them from animals. When science fiction includes aliens with hands that can perform delicate tasks, it is again distorting God's creation.

Other unique characteristics

There are other unique physical characteristics of man including a beautifully shaped body, fine skin, fine hair and the ability to produce a variety of facial expressions. When science fiction includes aliens who possess some or all of these characteristics, this detracts from the wonder of the human body and the uniqueness of man.

The following sections present a brief review of some specific science fiction stories/films to show how biblical doctrines are undermined.

[12.4] War of the Worlds by H G Wells

War of the Worlds is included in this chapter because it was the first popular science fiction story. Also, the story is still very popular today. The use of aliens in *War of the Worlds* is illustrated in the following extract:

'With infinite complacency men went to and fro over this little globe about their affairs, dreaming themselves the highest creatures in the whole vast Universe, and serene in their assurance of their empire over matter.... Yet across the gulf of space [Earth to the planet Mars] minds that are to our minds as ours are to those of the beasts that perish, intellects vast and cool and unsympathetic, regarded this Earth with envious eyes, and slowly and surely drew up their plans against us.'

Notice in this quotation how the fictitious aliens on Mars are portrayed as being more intelligent than human beings. The minds of the Martians are said to be superior to humans' in the same way that humans' are superior to the beasts'. The creation of Martians who are superior to humans represents a complete distortion of God's order of creation. Notice how

Wells says that humans were 'dreaming themselves the highest creatures in the whole vast Universe'. Here we can see that Wells is directly challenging the key biblical doctrine concerning the status of man as sole steward over creation. Many people might be tempted to view *War of the Worlds* as a harmless classic science fiction film. However, the story hinders people from having a true understanding of creation and so it must be considered unsuitable as entertainment.

(12.5) Star Wars

The original *Star Wars* theme appeared as a set of three films in the 1970s and 1980s and has been hugely popular. Recently, the *Star Wars* theme has been recreated with the film *Star Wars Episode I: The Phantom Menace*. The *Star Wars* films contain a large array of alien life forms, many of which have a spiritual dimension. There are also aliens who have some or all of the physical characteristics that are unique to man, including an intelligent mind, a sophisticated voice, an upright stature and agile hands. Children who have been brought up on films like *Star Wars* may well have problems appreciating that human beings are special creatures uniquely made in the image of God and uniquely designed to have a relationship with God and to have dominion over the created world.

Another problem with *Star Wars* is that it promotes false doctrines concerning the spiritual state of man. Bad characters like Darth Vader are portrayed as being completely evil, whilst good characters like Skywalker are portrayed as being wholly good. Such stereotypes undermine the truth of the gospel that every person has personal sin that needs to be dealt with. *Star Wars* also promotes the idea that physical beings in the Universe have the power to save the human race. There are often acts of salvation by 'superhero' people or 'superhero' aliens. There is no dependence on God or prayer to God.

The significant presence of supernatural powers is another negative aspect of *Star Wars*. There are several well-known scenes from *Star Wars* where the actors perform dramatic supernatural acts. In one scene, the villain Darth Vader decides to kill one of his own generals who has been disagreeable. To carry out the execution, he merely points at the general and causes a supernatural Force to strangulate him. Another example of a supernatural act occurs when the hero Skywalker is in danger of being killed and cannot reach his sword. In order to get the sword quickly, he merely stares at the weapon and causes it to move miraculously to his hand. As well as having these supernatural powers themselves, the characters are able to give the powers to others. One of the famous lines used in *Stars Wars* is 'may The Force be with you'. The frequent use of black magic in *Star Wars* presents a dangerously distorted view of the spiritual realm. The promotion of supernatural powers not only tempts people to meddle with black magic but it also prevents people from seeing the wonder of the powers of the Lord Jesus. Jesus has a miraculous ability to control nature and to heal people. When children read the Gospels, they should be filled with wonder at His power. However, after watching *Star Wars*, children may well think that the powers of the Lord Jesus are not particularly special.

Another problem with films like *Star Wars* is the idolatry given to the characters and the films. The release of the most recent series of *Star Wars* was accompanied by an enormous world-wide advertising campaign. It was difficult to buy cereals or take-away meals without *Star Wars* themes being plastered all over the packaging. Over the next decade a similar advertising campaign will no doubt be launched again. Children are especially vulnerable to such advertising because of their impressionable minds. Considering how *Star Wars* undermines so many key biblical doctrines, the films must be seen as unsuitable for Christians.

12.6 ET: The Extra Terrestrial

A very popular science fiction film appeared in 1982 called *ET*. In this film, a group of aliens visited the Earth in order to collect samples of the Earth's botanical life. After visiting a wooded area that was located near to a human settlement, one of the aliens was left behind. The alien was a web-footed creature with arms and fingers not unlike those of a human. After being left, the alien was found by a boy called Eliot, who then named the alien 'ET'. After becoming friends with the alien, Eliot hid ET in a cupboard until other aliens came back to collect him.

Many people consider the film *ET* as harmless entertainment. The fact that *ET* involves a friendship between an alien and children is seen as making the film particularly appropriate for the family. The film was a huge success with millions of videos sold and huge spin-off licences relating to video games, bicycles and other products for children.

Despite the popular view that *ET* is harmless family entertainment, there are several problems with the film. One of the dangers is the presence of supernatural powers such as a psychic attachment between Eliot and ET. When Eliot was hurt, ET was conscious of the injury and then supernaturally healed the boy. Another supernatural act occurred when ET was resurrected from the dead, seemingly by the power of love that Eliot had for the alien. Larson makes the following comment about *ET*:

'The most spiritually disturbing moment of the film took place as the two friends parted. ET pointed to the centre of Eliot's forehead and comforted his grieving friend with the consolation, 'I'll be right here'. I suspect that ET was pointing to the third eye, the presumed psychic centre of the telepathic perception. ET was telling Eliot that they could maintain their spiritually sympathetic communication even though galaxies apart. The theme of the movie was obvious: psychokinetic powers are superior to human faculties of speech and reason. I wonder how many children may have actually looked for extradimensional spiritual beings because of ET's message that the accumulated intelligence of the millennia and the supernatural powers of the occult reside in extraterrestrials?'[3]

The fact that films like *ET* are aimed at children is particularly worrying. Films like *ET* are officially rated as suitable for all ages, thus giving the impression of being harmless family entertainment. However, the reality is that they promote a false view of the physical and the spiritual worlds.

(12.7) Star Trek

Star Trek was first produced as a television series in the 1960s. It was a very successful series at the time and it continues to be successful in major film productions. The stories behind *Star Trek* movies usually involve a 'trek' in a spaceship called the *Enterprise* which travels from galaxy to galaxy, exploring the Universe. One of the main purposes of the exploration is to find extraterrestrial life. This is why the programmes started with the following words:

'Space...the final frontier. These are the voyages of the Starship Enterprise. Its five-year mission: to explore strange new worlds, to seek out new life and new civilisations - to boldly go where no man has gone before...'

Many people would regard *Star Trek* as harmless entertainment. This view is not surprising because *Star Trek* is certainly less harmful than many other films. The basic concept of exploring the Universe is one that easily and legitimately captures the imagination. However, despite these positive aspects, there remains a significant problem with *Star Trek* because alien life figures strongly in virtually all of the programmes.

(12.8) Other science fiction entertainment

There are quite a number of other science fiction films and series which could be shown to undermine important biblical doctrines. The television series *Dr Who* would be considered by many to be harmless. In one sense this is not surprising because the programme was designed for children and contained little violence or sex. However, even this series contained supernatural aspects such as the miraculous internal size of the Tardis and the supernatural travelling through space. In addition, various forms of aliens played a key role in the series.

Another area where there has been a large growth in science fiction is in computer games. One of the problems of computer games is their addictive nature. Many young children spend large amounts of their free time absorbed with the latest computer game. Apart from the problem of wasted time, there is the problem of exposure to the concept of alien life and supernatural powers.

(12.9) Wholesome science fiction

Is there any such thing as wholesome and legitimate science fiction? The answer to this question must be yes, although it is difficult to actually point to clear examples. A wholesome science fiction story must not undermine biblical doctrines. There must be no aliens and no evolutionary philosophy. There must be no human superheroes and no gross exaggeration of human powers. Of course, such constraints will sound incredibly boring to those who have been used to the extremes of *Star Wars* and *Star Trek*. However, this is the problem with science fiction. It is always trying to satisfy people's cravings for more and more sensational ideas.

12.10 Wholesome recreation

One of the sad aspects about children's interest in science fiction is that it often coincides with a lack of interest in God's creation, such as the stars in the night sky. Looking at the stars can seem so boring in comparison to the excitement of the latest science fiction film. And yet looking at the stars can actually be more exciting than any science fiction film. The Universe contains 'wonders without number' (Job 9:10). Even if we spent our whole life studying the stars, we would not be able to see everything that there was to see.

The Bible exhorts us to look up at the stars (Isaiah 40:26) because the stars have an important message to tell us. It can be very helpful for children to be shown the stars from a young age in order to develop a sense of wonder at God's creation. Fifty years ago it was common for children to be able to identify constellations such as Orion, the Plough and the Pleiades. However, modern children have little knowledge of or interest in the stars. Instead of knowing star patterns, modern children can identify many of the major characters in the big movie blockbusters. How we need to apply the words of the psalmist: 'Turn away my eyes from looking at worthless things' (Psalm 119:37). There is a great need today to encourage people to discover the stars. In the book of Job we are told: 'stand still and consider the wondrous works of God' (Job 37:14). How refreshing it is to stand outside at night and look at the beauty of the stars and to remember that these were made by the living God who now holds the Universe together by the word of His power (Hebrews 1:3).

Notes on Chapter 12

1   **Larson, B,** *UFOs and the Alien Agenda*, Nelson, p 209, 1997.
2   **Henry, M**, *Bible Commentary*, MacDonald Press, Vol. 3, Psalm 19:1, p. 301, 1710.
3   Ref 1, p 64.

Chapter 13

The united rebellion
of modern man

'Come, let us build ourselves a city, and a tower whose top
is in the heavens; let us make a name for ourselves...'
(Genesis 11:4).

M ankind has always rebelled against God. However, there are
times when man's rebellion is particularly fierce. One of the most
famous rebellions occurred at the Tower of Babel. This rebellion
was strong because man was united in language and ambition and was
therefore very powerful. In the modern age man is once again powerful
with global communication and trade. As at the time of Babel, modern
man uses this power to rebel against God in a very strong way. In particular,
the universal acceptance and teaching of evolution in schools and
Universities represents a united rebellion against God. Modern man also
seeks to bring glory to himself with ambitious projects on a global scale,
especially in the area of space exploration.

13.1 The rebellion at the Tower of Babel
The rebellion at the Tower of Babel is described in Genesis 11:

'Then they said to one another, "Come, let us make bricks and bake them
thoroughly". They had brick for stone and they had asphalt for mortar.
And they said "Come, let us build ourselves a city, and a tower whose top is
in the heavens; let us make a name for ourselves, lest we be scattered abroad
over the face of the whole Earth". But the Lord came down to see the city
and the tower which the sons of men had built. And the Lord said "Indeed
the people are one and they all have one language, and this is what they
begin to do; now nothing that they propose to do will be withheld from

them. Come, let Us go down and there confuse their language, that they may not understand one another's speech." So the Lord scattered them abroad from there over the face of all the Earth, and they ceased building the city' (Genesis 11:3-8).

There were three aspects to the rebellion at Babel:

❶ The united rejection of God
The people of Babel knew that God had commanded mankind to fill the whole Earth (Genesis 9:1). However, the people did not want to obey this command because it was safer and more convenient to remain at Babel. The rejection of God's commands amounted to a direct rebellion against God's authority. The fact that the people of Babel used the words 'let us' three times shows that the rebellion was united. The combined nature of the rebellion is also seen in the comment made by God: 'the people are one and they all have one language'. The people may also have had plans to worship other gods. The fact that the Tower was to reach the heavens shows that the Tower was probably intended to have a spiritual dimension.

❷ The control of man's destiny
Not only were the people disobeying God by staying in one place but they also thought they could positively prevent God from forcing them to spread out across the Earth. The people of Babel concluded that the building of a Tower would achieve the goal of preventing God from scattering them. This is why the people said 'lest we be scattered abroad over the face of the whole Earth'. The Tower would have helped to keep everyone together by providing a very significant focus for the city. Also, the very process of building the Tower would have had the effect of uniting all the people. The fact that the people of Babel really thought that they could prevent God from carrying out His purposes shows that the people of Babel had great confidence in their own power.

❸ The glorification of man
One of the purposes of the Tower of Babel was to bring glory to man. This is why the people said 'let us make a name for ourselves'. One of the reasons

why the Tower would bring glory to man was that it was going to be very tall. The fact that the bricks were to be baked thoroughly indicates that the tower was to be a very big structure. Also, the fact that the Tower was to reach the heavens shows that it was to be very tall. By building the biggest structure in the world, the people of Babel would have made themselves famous amongst men for many years. Even in the present age, man takes great pride in building the tallest structure in the world. Of course, the people of Babel did become famous, but not for the reason that they hoped for. The ambition of reaching heaven is interesting because the goal has now been achieved by man in the space age.

(13.2) The judgement at Babel

The fact that God came down to inspect the Tower shows that man's rebellion was a strong one. The main problem with the Tower was that it would unify people even more and increase their collective power. This is why God said: 'now nothing that they propose to do will be withheld from them'. God decided that the rebellion at Babel was serious enough for a world-wide judgement. The judgement involved the supernatural introduction of different languages so that the people would be confused.

The judgement was appropriate because the people had used their language to join together and rebel against God. Following the judgement at Babel, there would have been mistrust between different language groups and there would have been no possibility of a united rebellion against God. The judgement was also effective because there was such confusion of language that it was impossible to continue work on the Tower. Not only did the creation of languages stop the Tower from being built but it also forced the people to separate and hence spread across the world. Studies have shown that the world now has several thousand different languages. Even though many of these are closely related, we can deduce that there would have been many different languages created at the time of Babel.

In some ways the judgement at Babel has similarities with the judgement in the Garden of Eden and the judgement of the Flood at the time of Noah. In all three cases there was a rebellion by virtually the entire human race. In all three cases, the judgement applied to the entire (or virtually the entire) human race. And in all three cases, the judgement involved a supernatural action by God.

(13.3) The united rejection of God by modern man

We now live in a special age where the world has once again become a world-wide community in terms of communication and trade. Key recent events that have united the world include the formation of the United Nations, the formation of the World Trade Organisation and the end of the cold war. Major world projects like the International Space Station have also played an important role in uniting man. As well as living in a global community, we also live in an age of global communication. Technologies such as the World Wide Web and satellites make global communication relatively easy. There has not been such co-operation and communication on a world-wide scale since the Tower of Babel. Global co-operation and communications can, of course, be good. However, as they now exist, they are often used to rebel against God.

● The theory of evolution

One of the main ways in which modern man rebels against God is in his rejection of God as Creator. It is quite possible that the theory of evolution is 'the lie' which is referred to by the Apostle Paul in Romans 1. Paul refers to people who 'exchanged the truth of God for the lie, and worshipped and served the creature rather than the Creator'. Evolution is certainly a lie and it certainly does involve people worshipping the creation rather than the Creator.

The scientific community has established a united rejection of God as Creator. There is now little tolerance of anyone who does not hold to evolutionary belief. It is almost impossible to publish any criticisms about the theory of evolution in secular journals and conferences. Since the scientific community is now very integrated on a world-wide scale, all universities have a similar pro-evolution stance. The only exceptions are Christian institutions like the Institute for Creation Research in the United States. Whereas the people of Babel said 'Let us join together and build a tower', modern man has said, 'Let us join together and accept only man-made theories of origins'.

The rejection of God as Creator is clearly seen in the actions of the education authorities around the world. Biological evolution is now taught in biology classes and the Big Bang theory is taught in physics classes as 'facts' of science. The teaching of evolution as part of science curricula is particularly bad because this reinforces the view that evolution is a fact of science. In reality, evolution is only a man-made philosophy and should only ever be taught as part of religious education. There are pockets of resistance to the teaching of evolution, but these are only exceptions to the rule. There is also a strong bias towards evolutionary belief in the media and entertainment industries. Television programmes on astronomy present evolution as a fact of science and make no mention of God.

ⓘ Astrology

Another important way in which modern man rejects God is in the rejection of the Bible. Modern man has greater belief in astrology and horoscopes than in the Bible. Astrologers use the 12 constellations of the zodiac as twelve different star signs for people. Astrologers claim that the star sign that was current at your date of birth largely determines your character. Astrologers also claim that the position of stars and planets can be used to predict your future. Astrology is now very popular, with almost every magazine and newspaper containing daily or weekly horoscopes.

One interesting fact about astrology is that the star signs are out of date. The reason for this is that the Earth's axis slowly changes direction due to the gravitational pull of the Moon. The Earth's tilt does not change but the direction in which the axis points does change. The change in the Earth's axis is called precession and it takes about 26,000 years for the precession to complete one circle. Since the star signs were fixed a few thousand years ago, the constellations have moved relative to the Earth and appear at different times of the year compared to the corresponding star signs.

The falseness of astrology is described in Isaiah: 'Let now the astrologers, the stargazers, and the monthly prognosticators stand up and save you from these things that shall come upon you.' (Isaiah 47:13). This verse teaches that astrology and stargazing were false religions that would not help people at all in times of trouble. This is still true today. When people meet times of trouble, the advice given in horoscopes will be of no use whatsoever. The current widespread interest in astrology is a reflection of the stranglehold that Satan has on many people today.

The irony of man's rebellion

There are several ironic aspects to man's rebellion. These can be summarised as follows:

▶ Modern man is prepared to believe that cavities in a single meteorite present strong evidence of past life on Mars but is not prepared to believe that millions of living creatures give evidence of a Creator.

▶ Modern man is prepared to believe that the stars can tell us the future but not that there is a Creator who made the stars.

▶ Modern man is prepared to believe that supernatural powers are available to people but is not prepared to believe that God could have supernaturally created the world.

▶ Modern man is prepared to believe that aliens have visited the Earth and might visit again but is not prepared to believe that God sent Jesus Christ to the Earth and that Jesus will one day come again.

13.4 The control of man's destiny by modern man

Like the people of Babel, modern man is very determined to control his own destiny. However, there is a difference in the way modern man disobeys God. Whereas the people of Babel were determined to stay in one place, modern man is determined to form colonies of people on other planets. Since God has made the Earth specifically for man, both of these ambitions are wrong. Some scientists say that it is necessary to colonise other planets because the Earth will one day become uninhabitable due to lack of resources or some catastrophe such as a glacial period or global warming. However, the main reason why man wants to colonise other planets is that it will be seen as a great achievement by man.

The conversion of a barren planet like Mars into a habitable planet is being investigated by scientists from around the world. The goal of creating a habitable planet has been given the scientific term of 'terraforming'. Such an idea might sound far-fetched but terraforming is being seriously considered by scientists. In October 2000, NASA held a two-day workshop at the Ames Research Centre in California entitled *The physics and biology of making Mars habitable*. In this workshop the scientists discussed how it might be possible to produce an atmosphere on Mars. Ideas included the use of enormous mirrors to reflect the Sun's rays and melt the South Pole of Mars. Scientists at the meeting claimed that:

'drastic improvements in the life-sustaining characteristics of the environment of the Red Planet may be effected by humans using early to mid 21st century technologies...The spread of plants could produce enough oxygen to make Mars habitable within several millennia.'[1]

Recently, there has been the launch of a new high profile journal called the *International Journal of Astrobiology*.[2] This journal will publish papers on pre-biotic chemistry, planetary evolution, the search for extraterrestrial life and terraforming. Oberg has written a book entitled: *New Earth: Transforming other Planets for Humanity*,[3] and Fogg has written a journal paper on *Terraforming as part of a strategy for interstellar colonisation*.[4]

The ambition of colonising other planets was demonstrated recently in a NASA symposium on 40 years of American space flight held in Washington in May 2001. At the symposium the head of NASA, Daniel Goldin, said:

'We have been locked in Earth orbit for too long but we are going to break out. This civilisation is not condemned to live only on one planet. In our lifetimes, we will extend the reach of this human species on to other planets and to other bodies in our Solar System and build the robots that will leave our Solar System to go to other stars, then ultimately to be followed by people.'[5]

Over the next few decades it is very likely that the goals of finding extraterrestrial life and colonising other planets will become a major theme in science, education and entertainment. In his Genesis commentary, John

Calvin quotes a poet to describe how the people of Babel had an insane ambition:

'Man, rashly, daring, full of pride, most covets what is most denied, counts nothing arduous and tries insanely to possess the skies.'[6]

Modern plans to colonise Mars and other planets show that man still has the insane ambition of possessing the skies!

(13.5) The glorification of man in modern times

Like the people of Babel, modern man is very keen to bring glory to himself with great projects. An interesting parallel with the time of Babel is that many of these great projects are related to space. Whereas the people of Babel wanted to build a Tower that reached the heavens, modern man aims to colonise the heavens. Of course, there is nothing inherently wrong with space travel and space projects. There are many helpful space projects such as Earth observation satellites and communication satellites. However, some space projects are intended primarily to find evidence of evolution or to bring glory to man.

Space is now considered the 'final frontier' and the ultimate challenge for man. Tour guides at the Kennedy Space Centre in Florida now proclaim that 'with man nothing is impossible'. This kind of boast shows why God said at the time of Babel 'now nothing that they propose to do will be withheld from them'. There is now enough global co-operation between the rich nations of the world for man to indeed do almost anything he wants.

The importance of space programmes to man is shown in the amount of money spent on them. The annual space budget for NASA is of the order of $15 billion. The European and Japanese governments also spend very sizeable amounts of money on space missions. This money is spent on the space shuttle programme, the International Space Station, planetary probes and other space missions. A significant part of the money is spent on searching for life in space. Considerable finances are also spent on enabling humans to live in space, particularly in the International Space

Station. $15 billion is a huge sum of money. It is more than the entire annual gross national product of many countries including Kenya, Sri Lanka, Ghana and Zimbabwe.

A modern-day Tower of Babel

There are some remarkable parallels between the International Space Station (ISS) and the Tower of Babel. The assembly of the ISS has already started and it is due to be completed in 2005. A picture of what the ISS will look like when it is complete is shown in Figure 12. The ISS orbits the Earth just above the Earth's atmosphere. It will be much bigger than anything else that has been put into space, and will have a mass of about 500 tonnes whilst the solar arrays will cover an area of almost an acre. The space inside the ISS will be approximately the equivalent of two jumbo jets and it will be able to support up to seven people at any one time. Its vast size means that it will take many individual trips by the Space Shuttle to get all the parts of the ISS into space. In addition, the assembly will be a long and major operation.

The similarities with the Tower of Babel are summarised in Table 5. One similarity between the ISS and the Tower of Babel is that both have the purpose of getting humans into the heavens. The main purpose of a Space Station is to provide a continuous human presence on a structure at high altitude. This was demonstrated in the 1990s when the Russian Mir space station came to an end. When the last Russian cosmonaut left the Mir space station, he said, 'It is with grief in our hearts that we leave a piece of Russia'. It is very interesting that the ISS does reach into space. This shows that the ambition of the people of Babel was not so impossible after all.

Another similarity with the Tower of Babel is the world-wide co-operation. The ISS involves at least 16 nations: USA, Russia, Japan, 11 nations from Europe, Canada, and Brazil. Also, it is the first major international project in history to involve both the USA and Russia. This is because the project demands the technical expertise of all the major powers in the world. In particular, it is essential that the Russians participate because they already have the expertise to build the life-support systems. The Russians have proven this technology through their experience with the Mir space station.

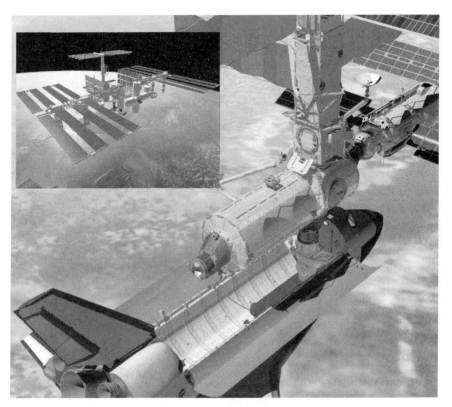

Fig. 12 Artist's impression of the Space Shuttle docking with the ISS
(Inset: how the completed space station will look on completion in 2005)

Another important similarity with the Tower of Babel is the cost of the project. The Tower of Babel would almost certainly have been the most costly project at that time if it had been completed. The ISS is also a record-breaking project. It will cost the order of $100 billion which makes it the biggest financial project in history. In fact, the project is so expensive that it can only take place if the USA, Europe and Japan combine their wealth.

Another similarity with the Tower of Babel is the unifying purpose. One of the important goals of the ISS is to unite different nations, especially the USA and Russia. The exploration of space is seen as an important way of unifying the nations of the world. One of the stated goals of NASA is as follows:

'NASA explores the Universe to enrich human life by stimulating intellectual curiosity, opening new worlds of opportunity, and uniting the nations of the world in this quest.'[7]

Another similarity between the Tower of Babel and the ISS is that there is no real necessity for the latter. Many scientists have pointed out that the experiments due to be performed on it could be carried out on other less expensive spacecraft. The ultimate reason why the ISS is going ahead is not because of any practical need but because of the way it unifies the nations of the world and because of the glory it brings to man.

TABLE 5 SIMILARITIES BETWEEN THE TOWER OF BABEL AND THE ISS

TOWER OF BABEL	INTERNATIONAL SPACE STATION
A tower	A manned structure at high altitude
Intended to reach the heavens	Does reach the heavens
World-wide project	First global space project
Largest project at time	Most expensive project in history
Unifying project	Project intended to unite world
No functional use	No real need for project

In John Calvin's commentary on the Tower of Babel, he comments on how man has a continual ambition to seek after his own glory:

'This is the perpetual infatuation of the world; to neglect heaven, and to seek immortality on Earth, where everything is fading and transient. Therefore, their cares and pursuits tend to no other end than that of acquiring for themselves a name on Earth.'[8]

This is exactly what man is like today. There is no regard for the things of God, but there is always a drive to bring glory to man.

(13.6) The judgement of God on modern man

At the time of the Tower of Babel God said: 'Indeed the people are one and they all have one language, and this is what they begin to do; now nothing that they propose to do will be withheld from them.' In modern times, man has again become very powerful and can do almost anything that he proposes to do. There is no reason to believe that man's current space projects will receive a special judgement in the way that the Tower of Babel did. However, it is still possible that God will not allow ungodly projects to prosper. In recent years there have been some unusual and spectacular failures of space missions which have been involved in searching for evidence of life on other planets. Some of the failures are described in Table 6.

When the first Russian Venus Lander reached that planet, the spacecraft experienced an embarrassing failure when the camera cap would not open to allow pictures to be taken. Having successfully got the spacecraft to Venus, scientists were distraught that such a simple problem prevented any pictures from being taken. But things went from bad to worse for the Russian scientists. After redesigning the camera cap and relaunching the Venus Lander, the camera ejected successfully but only to roll around the spacecraft and then roll right under the soil probe. The soil probe was designed to look for signs of life, but could only analyse the camera cap!

During the 1990s several major missions were planned for Mars that would carry out more investigations into the possibility of life on the planet. However, three of these missions ended in failure. The first of these missions was the Mars Observer spacecraft. This $1 billion spacecraft was launched in 1992 and was intended to commence orbiting Mars in 1993. However, before the spacecraft reached the planet, scientists lost contact with it due to a major technical fault, which was thought to be a leaking gas tank.

The second major mission to Mars which failed was the Mars Climate Orbiter, which was intended to reach its destination in 1999. Just before reaching Mars, the $125 million spacecraft was sent off course when scientists used the wrong units to navigate. The company that built the booster rockets provided navigational information in imperial units. However, NASA, who operated the spacecraft, assumed that the information was given in metric units. The end result of this embarrassing mistake was that the spacecraft was lost. A third major failure occurred on the $165 million Mars Polar Lander which was due to take soil samples.

Studies have shown that the switches used to control the engines as the spacecraft landed on the surface of Mars were faulty and this caused a catastrophic crash landing.

In total, NASA has had 13 missions to Mars and no fewer than five spacecraft have failed to make it to the planet in a working condition. Even more interesting is that the Soviet Union made 16 attempts to send spacecraft to Mars to search for life and all 16 failed![9] Many scientists have wondered how so many failures could have occurred in an age of supercomputers. It may be that the rebellious nature of man's projects provides the answer. When spacecraft are insured and when the environment is thought to have played a major part in the loss of the spacecraft, it is often the case that the insurance certificate states that the failure was due to an 'act of God'. It may be that failed missions to Venus and Mars really were due to an act of God!

TABLE 6   **FAILURES IN SPACECRAFT THAT HAVE BEEN SEARCHING FOR EXTRATERRESTRIAL LIFE**

SPACECRAFT	DATE	ORIGIN	FAILURE
Venera Venus lander	1970s	USSR	Camera cap would not detach
Venera 14 Venus lander	1981	USSR	Camera cap rolled under soil probe
Mars Observer	1993	NASA	Fuel leakage
Mars Climate Orbiter	1999	NASA	Wrong units used for navigation
Mars Polar Lander	1999	NASA	Engine problems during landing

(13.7) The judgement to come

It is remarkable how man does not learn from history. The lessons of the world-wide Flood and the Tower of Babel have not reformed man's behaviour because he still wants to wage war against God. The united rebellion of modern man may well be a sign that the next great judgement is shortly to come.

Notes on Chapter 13

1 Report in the Daily Telegraph, Monday 9 October, 2000.

2 Nature, *Insight section*, pp 1078-1122, 22 February, 2001.

3 **Oberg, JE,** *New Earths: Transforming Other Planets for Humanity*, Stackpole Books, 1981.

4 **Fogg, MJ,** *Terraforming as part of a strategy for interstellar colonisation*, Journal of the British Interplanetary Society, 44, pp 157-167.

5 Report in the Daily Telegraph, Thursday 10 May, 2001.

6 **Calvin, J,** *Genesis*, Banner of Truth Trust, Edinburgh, p 327, 1965.

7 NASA website.

8 Ref 6.

9 Report in Space flight, Vol 42, March 2000, p 93.

We are not alone!

'Seek the Lord while He may be found, call upon Him while He is near' (Isaiah 55:6).

14.1 We are not alone!

Over the last one hundred years there has been a constant desire amongst secular astronomers to build bigger telescopes in order to see further and further into the Universe. The main reason for wanting to see further has been to search for the ultimate origins of the Universe and to find out whether there is any extraterrestrial life. The Hubble Space Telescope represented a big step forward in the observational power of optical telescopes in the last decade. By being situated above the Earth's atmosphere, the telescope has been able to achieve a resolution of 0.1 arc second (less than one ten thousandth of a degree) which is the best resolution achieved so far. However, the Hubble Space Telescope has not got any closer to finding ultimate origins than any of the previous telescopes used to look at the stars. There are already plans to build a larger space telescope to replace the Hubble Space Telescope, but there is no reason to believe that this will provide any answers. No doubt telescopes will continue to become more powerful for years to come with man constantly hoping that they will give more understanding of the Universe.

One ironic aspect about man's use of large telescopes is that he refuses to listen to the voice of the stars. The further man looks into the Universe, the more clearly the stars speak of a Creator of infinite power and wisdom. And yet the further man looks, the more he refuses to believe that there is a God. Another ironic aspect about man's searching is that it is not necessary to look deep into space to find answers to ultimate questions. This is because the answers to the ultimate questions of life are found in the Bible. The Bible tells us who made the Universe, why it was made, how it was made, why man was made and what will happen in the future. Perhaps the biggest question that people would like answered is whether we are alone in the Universe. The Bible teaches that we are not alone because there is a God who is real.

To find God it is not necessary to point powerful telescopes towards the edges of the Universe. Rather, we can find God by pointing our hearts in the right direction. In the Bible, in the prophecy of Jeremiah, God says to us, 'You will seek Me and find Me when you search for Me with all your heart' (Jeremiah 29:13). The Bible also teaches that God is near to each one of us. The Apostle Paul tells us: 'God, who made the world and everything in it… has made from one blood every nation of men to dwell on all the face of the Earth, and has determined their preappointed times and the boundaries of their habitation, so that they should seek the Lord, in the hope that they might grope for Him and find Him, though He is not far from each one of us' (Acts 17:24-27).

14.2 A visit from heaven

Many people wonder whether the Earth has ever been visited by beings from outer space. The Bible teaches that there has already been a special visit from heaven. The visit was not by aliens but by God's Son, the Lord Jesus Christ. Two thousand years ago, He was miraculously conceived in the womb of a virgin mother. He was born in the land of Israel and worked as a carpenter before preaching the good news of the gospel. The purpose of the visit is described in the Gospel of John: 'For God so loved the world, that He gave His only begotten Son, that whosoever believes in Him shall not perish but have everlasting life.' (John 3:16). The Bible teaches that all people are sinners (Romans 3:23) and that our natural state is one of rebellion against God. The only way that a person can have a relationship with God is by repenting of their sins and trusting in the Lord Jesus Christ. The reason why we must have faith in Jesus Christ is that He lived a perfect life and paid the price for the sins of His people on the cross of Calvary. When we trust in Christ, God forgives our sin and counts Christ's righteousness on our behalf. Those who trust in Him will one day live in heaven for eternity with God.

The stars can remind us of the special status of the Lord Jesus Christ. He is the One who created the world, the One who has redeemed the world and the One who will judge the world. In the book of Revelation we read: 'I am the Alpha and the Omega, the Beginning and the End, the First and the

Last... I am the Root and Offspring of David, the Bright and Morning Star' (Revelation: 22: 13 & 16). The morning star is the planet Venus because it is so bright that it can be seen after sunrise when all the other stars have disappeared from view. The uniqueness of the planet Venus in the morning sky reminds us of the uniqueness and supremacy of the Lord Jesus Christ. The morning star can also remind us that the Lord Jesus is the light that shines in the darkness of the world (John 1:5).

14.3 A reminder of God's promises in the stars

The stars remind us of some of the great promises in the Bible. They include:

❶ A reminder of God's mercy

The psalmist tells us: 'For as the heavens are high above the Earth, so great is His mercy toward those who fear Him' (Psalm 103:11). The great distance to the stars helps to reinforce the truth that God is very merciful to His people. Our natural state of rebellion against God and His law is such that we do not deserve forgiveness. But God's mercy is so great that He is merciful to anyone who repents. The nearest star is approximately 40 thousand billion km away. And yet there are about 100 billion other stars in our galaxy that are even further away, and billions of other galaxies of stars that are further still. In the same way that these distances are vast, so the magnitude of God's mercy is great. Another verse that reminds us of God's great mercy is found in Nehemiah: '...though some of you were cast out to the farthest part of the heavens, yet I will gather them from there...' (Nehemiah 1:9). When we think of the great distances to the stars we can be reminded of the great magnitude of God's mercy.

❷ A reminder of God's people

In Genesis we read of God's promise to Abraham: '...Look now toward heaven, and count the stars if you are able to number them...so shall your descendants be' (Genesis 15:5). The word 'descendants' here does not mean the literal descendants of Abraham but people who will trust in the same God with the same faith. The promise made to Abraham is that there will be so many people who come to know God that it will be impossible for anyone to number them. To illustrate this promise, God uses the analogy of counting the stars. When we consider the great number of stars, we can be reminded of God's gracious promise to Abraham. The promise can be a tremendous encouragement because it shows that the number of people who will go to heaven has not been restricted to a small number. It is interesting to note that the stars we see today are the same as those seen by Abraham and are the same stars that will be seen by future generations. This reminds us that the promise made to Abraham is still valid today and will be for all time.

⓲ A reminder of the future glory of God's people
The stars also remind us of the future glory of God's people. The Bible says: 'Those who are wise shall shine like the brightness of the firmament, and those who turn many to righteousness like the stars forever and ever' (Daniel 12:3). In the same way that the stars have a glorious brightness, so God's people will have a glorious brightness when in heaven.

(14.4) A great salvation
In Psalm 8 we read how the stars are the work of God's fingers. In contrast, the Bible teaches that God has saved His people with the strength of His arm (Psalm 77:15). Of course, these passages are using metaphorical language because God does not carry out work with physical fingers and arms. However, the terms do emphasise that God's work of salvation was an even greater work than the creation of the stars. God's purposes in the Universe and His power to save are wonderfully summarised in the following verses:

'For thus says the Lord, who created the heavens, who is God, who formed the Earth and made it, who has established it, who did not create it in vain, who formed it to be inhabited: "I am the Lord, and there is no other…Look to Me and be saved, all you ends of the Earth! …"' (Isaiah 45:18 & 22).

The Creator of the Universe invites people of all nations to look to Him for salvation. Any reader who does not know the Creator of the Universe is urged to seek Him and His forgiveness.

Physical properties of the Solar System

Table A.1
Properties of the Sun

Mass M (kg)	Diameter D (km)	Power P (W)	Surface temperature (K)	Temperature near centre (K)
1.99×10^{30}	1,394,000	3.9×10^{26}	6,000	15 million

Notes on power numbers:

$\times 10^{30}$ means that the decimal point must be moved 30 places to the right.

1.99×10^{30} = 1,990,000,000,000,000,000,000,000,000,000

1.99×10^{30} = 1.99 thousand billion billion billion

Notes on temperature:

K = degrees Kelvin

0° C = 273 K

How does the Sun produce energy?

The Sun consists mainly of hydrogen (about 70%) and helium (about 28%). There are two main theories of how the Sun produces energy. One is nuclear fusion and the other is gravitational collapse. Most scientists believe that nuclear fusion takes place in the centre of the Sun with the conversion of hydrogen to helium. Energy from this reaction is thought to move outwards through radiative and convective zones to the surface where it is given off as light and heat. If nuclear fusion is taking place, then the proportion of helium will gradually increase over time. The evidence concerning nuclear reactions in the Sun is inconclusive. Nuclear fusion should produce a large number of sub-atomic particles called neutrinos but these have not been detected in sufficient quantities to provide convincing evidence of nuclear reactions. Gravitational collapse is based on the idea that the Sun is collapsing under its own gravity and that potential energy is converted into kinetic motion of particles thus releasing large amounts of energy. The evidence for gravitational collapse is also inconclusive. It may be that either or both of the methods described above are responsible for the generation of energy in the Sun.

Table A.2

Properties of the planets in the Solar System

Planet	Mass M (kg)	Diameter D (km)	Average distance from Sun r (million km)	Orbital period T (years)	Number of moons
MERCURY	3.30×10^{23}	4,880	57.9	0.24	0
VENUS	4.87×10^{24}	12,100	108	0.62	0
EARTH	5.98×10^{24}	12,750	150	1	1
MARS	6.42×10^{23}	6,800	228	1.88	2
JUPITER	1.90×10^{27}	139,000*	778	11.9	16
SATURN	5.69×10^{26}	114,000*	1,430	29.5	18
URANUS	8.69×10^{25}	51,100	2,870	84.0	15
NEPTUNE	1.02×10^{26}	49,500	4,500	164.8	8
PLUTO	1.32×10^{22}	2,320	5,910	248.5	1

* average

Appendix A

Table A.3
Properties of large moons in the Solar System*

Moon	Mass M	Diameter D	Average distance to planet r	Orbital period T	Planet
	(kg)	(km)	(000 km)	(days)	
THE MOON	7.35×10^{22}	3,480	384	27.3	Earth
IO	8.93×10^{22}	3,630	422	1.77	Jupiter
EUROPA	4.80×10^{22}	3,140	671	3.55	Jupiter
GANYMEDE	1.48×10^{23}	5,260	1,070	7.15	Jupiter
CALLISTO	1.08×10^{23}	4,800	1,880	16.7	Jupiter
TITAN	1.35×10^{23}	5,150	1,220	16.0	Saturn
TRITON	2.14×10^{22}	2,710	355	5.9	Neptune

* these are the only moons that are larger than the planet Pluto

Exercises in astronomy and physics

General questions

1. Which is the largest planet?
2. Which is the largest moon?
3. How many moons are larger than Pluto?
4. How many moons are larger than Mercury?
5. How many moons are heavier than Pluto?
6. How many moons are heavier than Mercury?
7. How many times larger (in diameter) is the Sun than the Earth?
8. How many times heavier is the Sun than the Earth?
9. How many times larger (in diameter) is Jupiter than the Earth?
10. How many times heavier is Jupiter than the Earth?

Calculation of surface area, volume and density

The surface area, S of a sphere can be calculate from the following formula:

$$S = 4 \pi R^2 \ (m^2)$$

where R is the radius of the sphere in metres ($R = D/2$)

The volume, V of a sphere can be calculated from the formula:

$$V = \frac{4}{3} \pi R^3 \ (m^3)$$

The density of a body is defined as the average level of mass per unit volume. To calculate density it is necessary to know the mass, M and volume, V of the body. Density, ρ can be calculated form the following formula:

$$\rho = \frac{M}{V} \ (kg/m^3)$$

QUESTIONS

❶ Calculate the surface area of each planet.
❷ Calculate the volume of each planet.
❸ Calculate the density of each planet.
❹ Which planet has the highest density?
❺ Which planet has the lowest density?

EXERCISE 3
Calculation of weight

The weight of an object on the surface of a planet is dependent on the size of the planet. The weight, W of an object can be calculated from the following formula:

$$W = m\,g \quad \text{(N)}$$

where m = mass of object in kg
g = acceleration due to gravity in m/s^2

The acceleration due to gravity, g at the surface of a planet or moon can be calculated from Newton's law of gravitation as follows:

$$g = \frac{GM}{R^2}$$

where G = 6.67 x 10^{-11} Nm^2/kg^2
M = mass of planet or moon in kg
R = radius of planet or moon in metres

QUESTIONS

❶ Calculate g for the Earth, the Moon and Mars.
❷ How much would a 100 kg object weigh on the Earth, the Moon and Mars?

EXERCISE 4
Calculation of orbital velocity of man-made satellites

A man-made satellite is kept in orbit by gravitational attraction and orbital motion. The satellite must have an orbital velocity such that the centripetal acceleration of the satellite in circular motion is the same as the gravitational acceleration acting on the satellite. Many man-made satellites orbit the Earth at about 300 km above the Earth's surface.

The centripetal acceleration, a of a satellite in circular orbital motion can be calculated from the following formula:

$$a = \omega^2 r \quad (\text{m/s}^2)$$

where ω = angular velocity of satellite around the Earth in r/s
       r = distance between satellite and centre of the Earth in metres

The gravitational acceleration, g between a satellite and the Earth can be calculated from the formula:

$$g = \frac{GM}{r^2} \quad (\text{m/s}^2)$$

where G = 6.67 x 10^{-11} Nm^2/kg^2
      M = mass of the Earth in kg
      r = distance between satellite and centre of the Earth in metres

By combining the above two equations, the orbital velocity of a satellite can be calculated from the following formula:

$$\omega = \left[\frac{GM}{r^3}\right]^{1/2} \quad (\text{r/s})$$

Appendix B

The time period, T of a satellite can be calculated from the following formula:

$$T = \frac{2\pi}{(60\omega)} \quad \text{(minutes)}$$

The linear velocity, v of a satellite can be calculated from the following formula:

$$v = \omega r \frac{3600}{1000} \quad \text{(km/hour)}$$

QUESTIONS

❶ Calculate the time period of a satellite that has an altitude of 300 km above the Earth's surface.

❷ Calculate the linear velocity of the satellite in question [1].

❸ Calculate the time period (in hours) of a satellite that is 35,900 km above the Earth's surface.

❹ What is special about the time period of the satellite in question [3]?

ANSWERS to exercises

EXERCISE 1

1. Jupiter
2. Ganymede
3. 7
4. 2
5. 7

6. o
7. 109
8. 333,000
9. 11
10. 318

EXERCISE 2

Planet	S (m²)	V (m²)	Density ρ (kg/m³)
MERCURY	7.48×10^{13}	6.08×10^{19}	5420
VENUS	4.60×10^{14}	9.28×10^{20}	5250
EARTH	5.12×11^{14}	1.09×10^{21}	5510
MARS	1.45×10^{14}	1.65×10^{20}	3900
JUPITER	6.07×10^{16}	1.41×10^{24}	1350
SATURN	4.08×10^{16}	7.76×10^{23}	730
URANUS	8.20×10^{15}	6.99×10^{22}	1240
NEPTUNE	7.70×10^{15}	6.35×10^{22}	1610
PLUTO	1.69×10^{13}	6.54×10^{18}	2020

4. Highest density = Earth
5. Lowest density = Saturn

EXERCISE 3

Body	Gravity g (m/s^2)	Weight W (N)
EARTH	9.81	981
MOON	1.62	162
MARS	3.7	370

EXERCISE 4

1. 90.4 minutes
2. 27,800 km/hour
3. 24 hours
4. 24 hours is a geo-stationary orbit because the rate of rotation is equal to the rate of rotation of the Earth. A geo-stationary satellite can orbit the Earth such that it continually stays above the same geographical location. Geo-stationary satellites are particularly convenient for communication because they are in permanent contact with the same geographical location.

Chapter 1

GROWING FOR GOD

Simon Robinson

80 pages A5 PB   £3.99

1 903087 26 0

When we were children the people who cared about us were very concerned for our development. They would measure our height, check our weight, and regulate our diet, because they knew the importance of physical growth. The New Testament places the same kind of emphasis on spiritual growth. It tells us to 'leave the elementary teachings about Christ and go on to maturity', (Hebrews 6:1). And to 'grow up in our salvation' (1 Peter 2:2). This is never suggested, but always commanded. 'Growing for God' is a book that takes these commands seriously. It looks at this great subject in the context of God's plan for our lives, encouraging us to grow for His glory and provides practical instruction which will help us to achieve this goal.

REFERENCE: GFG

Scripture regularly instructs us to employ the means of spiritual growth, and to pursue maturity in Christlikeness. Simon Robinson's Growing for God is a valuable handbook for all who seek to obey those imperatives

JOHN MACARTHUR

THE TEN COMMANDMENTS FOR TODAY

Brian H. Edwards

288 pages A5 PB   £8.99

0 902548 69 7

At a time when the nation's morality is in alarming decline, it is surprising that so little has been written on the Ten Commandments. Brian Edwards gives us a modern commentary, carefully uncovering their true meaning, and applying them incisively to our contemporary society.

REFERENCE: 1OT

"Brian Edwards' book finds a well deserved place at the cutting edge of application of this important theme"

THE BANNER OF TRUTH MAGAZINE

RESPONDING TO THE CULTURE OF DEATH

John R Ling

128 pages A5 PB   £5.99

1 903087 26 0

Most people are confused about 'new' bioethical issues such as human cloning and genetic engineering. Many have not even thought through the 'old' bioethical issues like, abortion and euthanasia.
The author's conviction is that we now live in a culture of death. Much of modern medicine has gone seriously wrong, and now it has become a threat to all men, women, and children.
This book does not seek to give trite, comfortable answers. Rather it develops a rugged bioethical framework, based on principles derived from the Bible, and supported by analyses of recent trends in medicine and science. But this book is not simply about cosy, fireside casuistry. It wants you out of your armchair and doing—it calls for a response of 'principled compassion' to overcome this culture of death and gain the culture of life.

REFERENCE: RCD

ON GIANTS' SHOULDERS

Edgar Powell

280 pages A5 PB   £8.99

0 902548 93 X

If you are usually put off by any book which describes itself as an apologetic, and yet long to arm yourself with facts to respond to the evolutionists, you may find this book helpful. Christians are used to being told that they need 'religion' as a form of security in this uncertain life. In fact, it takes courage and conviction to stand up for the Gospel!
Written by Edgar Powell, *On Giants' Shoulders* responds vigorously to the propaganda from the evolutionists by providing thought-provoking answers. Thoroughly recommended.

REFERENCE: GS

"A splendid overview of contemporary apologetic challenges"

CHRISTIANITY TODAY (USA)

"Edgar Powell has done the church a great service by his careful, gracious and winsome presentation."

EVANGELICAL TIMES

"...an outstanding achievement...food for thought on every page"

PROFESSOR WILLIAM EDGAR,
WESTMINSTER THEOLOGICAL SEMINARY,
PHILADELPHIA

Also from Day One